Talking and Thinking Floorbooks™

GW00537467

Using 'Big Book Planners' to consult children.

by Claire Warden

Many thanks to all the children and adults who have made this book possible.
Special thanks to Kildrum Nursery Centre, who believed in my approach
and supported me from the beginning.

© Claire Warden 1994
First published 2006

The rights of Claire Warden to be identified as the author of this work have been asserted in accordance with the Copyright Designs and Patents Act 1988.

Design and layout by Jan Vickers 2006
© Photography by Claire Warden & Nicki Buchan 2006

ISBN 0-9544883-6-9

Talking and Thinking Floorbook™, Talking Tub™, Talking Tree™ and Talkaround Mat™ are all terms created by Claire Warden. Please acknowledge this when using the approach.

If you would like training materials or in-service on this book, please contact Mindstretchers.

Mindstretchers
The Warehouse
Rossie Place
Auchterarder
Perthshire
PH3 1AJ

Tel/Fax: 01764 664409
www.mindstretchers.co.uk

Foreword

The elements that have become known as the 'Mindstretchers approach' started out as a strategy to encourage oracy in the early years. In the areas where I worked at the very start of my career, there were children whose emotional intelligence was low and therefore their perception of themselves was as individuals with little worth or status. The oracy skills of these children were limited with a number choosing to be mute. Their personal motivation had been switched off. The three aspects combined together to necessitate an approach that was very child centred, focused on motivation, was sensorial to encourage engagement and was not over steered by the pressure of time.

Children's thinking and their needs, rather than those of the adults were put at the centre of our work. The environment was very rich in every type of stimulation and children were given time to develop their own thinking at their own pace. It is an approach that has stayed with me wherever I have worked.

It is this approach that seems to be gathering momentum and sparking educators across the country. In response to their requests I have put together this book to explain the thinking behind the approach I use. I do hope that it helps people to celebrate the variety of high quality experiences available to children and their carers.

Some people talk to me about citizenship, others of personal learning plans, many enjoy the nature of children's thinking and seeing how the approach encourages progression and deeper learning. Many aspects will overlap with identified approaches such as Montessori, High scope, and traditional 'good practice'. Each idea on its own has value, but when they come together they seem to be switching adults and young children on to learning, which is wonderful news.

I would like to thank everyone who has shared their thinking with me, because they have undoubtedly affected the way I work. The 'people' are from 0-82 years old and I feel enriched by the process of heated debate or gentle affirmation. If you would like to chat about the contents of this book I would love to hear from you. The contact is on the inside cover.

Contents

Introduction   1

Thinking about the brain   3

     What is a Talking and Thinking Book ?   9

First Steps   A new way of working   11

     Introducing the book

     Big floorbooks

     Making the book

Starting points   Child initiated - Case study - The Little House   15

     Adult initiated - Case study - The Bird Hide

Encouraging children to tell you what they think   23

     Ethos

     Effective questioning

Talking tubs™   25

     Use of 3D objects

     Use of 2D materials

Three Dimensional mind mapping - Case study - Water   29

Meetings & group discussions - Case study - Spoons   35

Group writing - Case study - The Body Book   41

Supporting individuals - Case study - A Windy Day   45

Talking & thinking trees™ - Case study - Numeracy   51

Consultation boards - Indoors and Out   59

Consulting children within routines   61

Gathering opinion - Voting systems   63

Consulting about knowledge - Case study - Electricity   65

Consulting about design & layout - Case study - Outdoor Areas   67

Consulting about display - Case study - Morrison's Crocodile   69

Consulting about resources - Case study - An outdoor den   71

Eco Nurseries, the consultation process   73

The long term perspective - Is it sustainable ?   75

Facing the challenges   77

Bibliography and further reading   79

Inside & Outside

- Talking & Thinking Tree™

- Observation

- Photos - P.L.O.D.S. (Possible Lines of Development)

- 3D Mind map

- Consultation boards
  - blank
  - selection of photographs

- Talking & Thinking Floorbook™

- Develop knowledge through interest

- Creative plans

- Balance of emotional intelligence and I.Q.

- Fun

- Maintains spontaneity

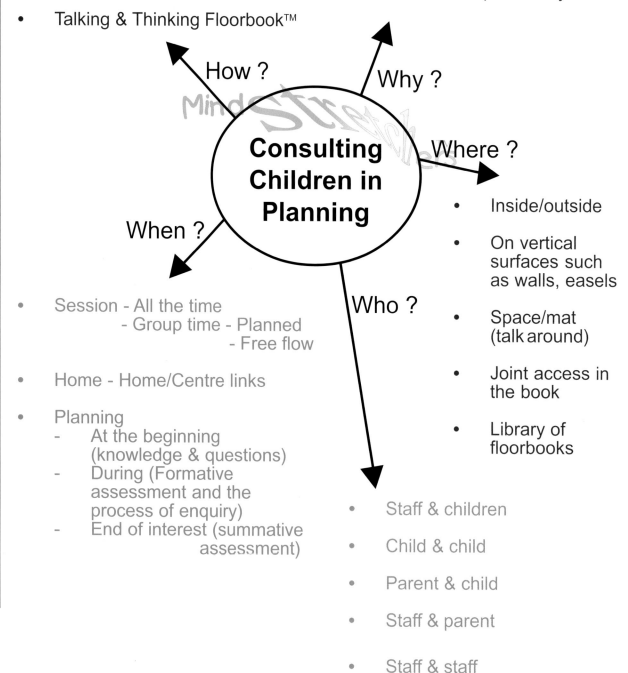

How ?

Why ?

Where ?

When ?

Who ?

Consulting Children in Planning

- Inside/outside

- On vertical surfaces such as walls, easels

- Space/mat (talk around)

- Joint access in the book

- Library of floorbooks

- Session - All the time
  - Group time - Planned
  - Free flow

- Home - Home/Centre links

- Planning
  - At the beginning (knowledge & questions)
  - During (Formative assessment and the process of enquiry)
  - End of interest (summative assessment)

- Staff & children

- Child & child

- Parent & child

- Staff & parent

- Staff & staff

All of the documents that we use in early education across the UK talk about the issues that are going to be explored in this book. Areas covered include 'child centred planning', 'autonomy', 'citizenship', 'personal learning plans', 'evidence of group progression', 'building on what they know', 'greater involvement in planning' and motivation.

'Thinking, talking & recording'

It would appear, from the training across the United Kingdom, that people are aware of what they want to do, but lack a clear methodology to achieve it. The Talking and Thinking Floorbook™ has been adopted by many centres to support child initiated planning. They are being used in Primary one and two classrooms to develop thinking skills.

The DFEE have created the foundation stage guidelines for England and Wales and have based them on certain principles. These principles state that practitioners are required to 'plan and organise the learning environment to provide experiences that build on what children already know'.

This will be demonstrated when practitioners 'enable children to become involved by planning experiences which are mostly based on real life situations'

These relevant real life situations come out through the Talking & Thinking Floorbook™ as part of the consultation process.

In a project called the Effective Provision for Pre-School Education (E.P.P.E.) they looked at the way that children use skills in contexts that are meaningful to them. In the creation of a munching monster that had tubes running through it the author states: *'This idea came from the children and they measured it up and developed it. The biggest problem came with trying to attach the cardboard tubes to the wall. In this way we became involved in shared thinking'*

When the E.P.P.E project looked at different types of experience they found that this type of thinking was particularly important in developing and extending concepts. The group writing in a Talking & Thinking Floorbook™ explores the shared thinking in a more formal way so that children recall each others ideas and record them through writing, diagrams and photographs. Many children re-visit the books and learn from a previous groups experience or indeed their own ideas from a previous session.

'Children recording ideas on bubbles that can then go in the floorbook'

When children engage with an adult and discuss their ideas and thoughts they are entering into a partnership to 'find out'. Fisher (1996) states -
'If children know that they are being trusted and are being given the opportunity to make their own choices and decisions then they also know, because it is part of a negotiation

made explicit by the teacher, that they have to fulfil their side of the bargain.' P143

Recording the elements of the 'negotiation' allows children to remind themselves and the adult what they have agreed to do. Talking & Thinking Floorbooks™ create a child centred approach, which records the evidence of the process of play and the learning that comes from it.

Writing thoughts down

The approach is made up of a number of facets that are outlined in the following chapters. To support people who, like myself, work more effectively in a diagrammatic way, I have created a mind map that outlines the book and therefore the approach I take (ref Page iv). The strategies are all interlinked and can be used when the adults feel the time is right.

The right to be consulted, and subsequently empowered to make decisions, lies at the heart of the way I work.

Consultation with children is important because;
- it creates a closer match between the child and the curriculum it is experiencing.
- it builds self esteem and positive attitudes when the learner is involved in the decision making.
- it increases intrinsic motivation, that stays with a child throughout life.
- children have a right to be treated with respect. As individuals, we can show respect by valuing their thoughts and opinions.

'Stars are from Asda' - children's ideas

The initial thoughts, evidence of the process of play and a summary of ideas are collated in a Talking and Thinking Floorbook™.

Talking and Thinking FloorBooks™ have evolved in my practice over the last 20 years in response to working with children in a variety of environments. When they were initially used we called them floorbooks because we made them with children on the floor, they then moved into the planning frame and were known as Big Book planners! The term I now use is a 'Talking and Thinking Floorbook™' since it reflects their purpose, which is to encourage thinking skills through talking and listening together in a group, so that children are consulted and can then influence the opportunities taking place.

Talking and Thinking Floorbooks™

- Brain based approaches are making our interactions more informed
- Many theories blend together to give an holistic picture
- Awareness of our own learning style helps us to understand our style of working, those of our team and the children we work with.

"Is it dark in my head?"…"No! 'cos if it was your brain couldn't read"
Two children age 5

When I started to work in education I had trained with a clear knowledge of theory and the theorist, but when I was playing and working with children I found myself asking, 'Why do they do that ?' 'How can I motivate him ?' 'Why are those children approaching the same task in a different way ?'
Now we have evidence of the way we learn due to improved neurological understanding. The advances in technology over the last 10 years, through Magnetic Resonance Imaging Scans and Computerised Axial Tomography which can actually scan brains and show learning paths means that we are beginning to understand the way the brain works. It is still very new and I would urge readers to hold on to the broad beliefs put forward in this book because the detail may well develop.

Kotulak (1997) states
'When it comes to building the human brain, nature supplies the construction materials and nurture serves as the architect that puts them together'

The debate between nature and nurture is an ongoing one. This section is designed to start the process of adult reflection, to think about the children and adults we work with. I have included anecdotal tales to encourage you to reflect on your own peculiarities.

The brain is wonderfully complex and any simple way that I am able to describe it will undoubtedly be full of inaccuracy to a neuroscientist!!
These are the aspects that seem to influence my work the most and I can see evidence of them when I work with young children. It is these aspects that I will describe here and recommend readers refer to the bibliography for more detailed analysis and research.

Multi-tasking

At approximately 6-8 weeks in utero a hormone was released into the brain that began to create two hemispheres with a membrane called the Corpus Callosum. The membrane works like a super highway between the hemispheres. But its structure seems to be different in different types of brain. The effectiveness of this membrane affects how we approach learning and how readily we can multi-task.
There are people who can put the washing on, cook and read a book all at the same time. There are also people who will put the washing on, then cook, then read a book rather than doing them all the same time. The ability to multi-task has been seen to be partly due to the structure of the Corpus Callosum. Put very simply a female orientated brain seems to have an increased number of connections crossing from left to right, therefore using all aspects of the brain. Male orientated brains have fewer of those connections and generally do not multi-task as effectively. Children in our centres behave in this way. One child will flit from area to area taking bits of junk to the

construction area, masking tape from the writing zone and ultimately put together his television in the role play area. Other children go to an area and wish to stay there until they have finished a personal task. In response to this we need to be flexible about the way we organise our play areas. There need to be a number of times and places that children are consulted in order to focus planning. If we say it will only happen at a set time, many of the multi-tasking children may not be involved.

Hemisphere Dominance.

Using the whole of your brain with all its facets is clearly the most effective for learning. There are two hemispheres in the brain and they are seen to be associated with different aspects of learning The left brain, logical, precise, analytical, sequential, discrete information, ordered. The right brain creative visualisation, random, responsive, contextual, explores the big picture, finds patterns and connections. There is clearly a difference in the way that people approach tasks even down to the way that they record notes, or organise their cupboards. People who have met me are aware of my right brain dominance with characteristics such as random thinking that makes my notes appear in a way that resembles a mind map. The preference I show for contextual learning is in the stories that I tell, my creativity in the way I choose to use sensorial materials in very open ways. They create the way I prefer to work, an approach that seems natural to me.

My partner however has a different approach to order and structure. Catalogues full of boxes and things to sort into them inspires him! Learning is recorded in bullet pointed lists of information rather than creative doodles. When our children came along it appeared that they also had what seemed to be a predisposition that affected the way they approached tasks. If we take writing, one child was inspired by swirly paper, with little structure cut into abstract shapes, the other reached for squared paper cut into regular shapes. After years of working with young children I believe that people are on

a continuum, some enjoying structure and functionality more than others. When I work with children I now consider the resources I provide, even down to the range of paper I provide for the talking and thinking bubbles. If we keep an element of this idea in our minds it offers an explanation why, given free choice, some children go towards construction and others go towards creative fabrics. We can use this knowledge to adjust our environment in simple ways to perhaps move baskets of soft toys to the construction to provide a more creative context for building.

In case you are considering this aspect to be gender specific, I would like to say that I don't believe that it is. I have met and worked with females who are very precise, ordered and sequential.

People do move around on the continuum and individuals are affected by a range of other environmental factors. To put yourself in a box limits your potential, using the whole of your brain will remove the boundaries.

Gathering the information

It was with some interest that I used to read lesson plans as a lecturer and ponder to myself how I would react to the session as a child. The plans identified a balance of physical, practical and recorded activities in each session but lacked sensorial experiences embedded in kinaesthetic activities. The use of adult designed materials in single plastic colours limits children's thinking skills. For example when you close your eyes and visualise a group of yellow plastic resources, they seem to have the same colour 'lot number' that creates little variety. Imagine then, the potential of yellow rose petals to engage children. As practitioners we know the research but often find it hard to put it into practice given the parameters of the work place. On closer inspection the visual learners seemed to have a lot, but the auditory, tactile, and movement based learners had far less. So through a variety of project work we began to promote heuristic materials. The effect was greater engagement and more stimulating conversations. It was this aspect that led to the creation of Bags of Discovery™, Talking Tubs™ and all the resources that we now promote.

Learning styles

Learning styles have recently been classified by people such as Alasdair Smith (2001) to three main areas Visual, Auditory and Kinaesthetic. This does make the process more manageable and can encourage people in Primary Schools to look at their style of teaching and learning. However the tactile element of the work I do with very young children should perhaps be held as a separate area, rather than embedding it into general kinaesthetics. Young children do mouth and handle a variety of materials but the place of taste, texture and smell are as important as sight and sound in our youngest children.

Smith and Call (2003) suggest that;

- ❖ The visual learners learn more effectively through pictures, diagrams, moving images, colour and watching a process.
- ❖ The Auditory learners learn more effectively through hearing sound, voices and rhythm
- ❖ Kinaesthetic learners learn by experiencing in a practical way, through doing, moving and touching.

When we look at the effect of this on young children we can begin to identify how important it is to be aware of strategies such as 3D mindmapping, storytelling and the use of large spaces such as outside, so that all children are given a channel to discover and learn in a way that suits them.

The Filing Cabinet

Fascination with real objects

Inside our brain I like to visualise a magnificent storage facility. All of our memories and experiences are passed through the brain, some are only stored in the short term, but those that have an emotional link to us are stored away for later retrieval. The Neo Cortex acts like a processing unit and can attempt to access the information. When asked a simple question such as 'what do you know about rabbits?' the brain has an immediate choice … forward or not. Children of three have a great deal of information in the ' filing cabinet,' but sometimes it is related to what adults might view as the detail. Having searched through this incredible storage facility it can bring forward information. When young children talk to us, they do so in their way, exploring words and trying to develop an understanding of the world. The quote at the start of this section is an example. At the start of the learning process children are positive about the potential of the world and the way that it works. It makes perfect sense to a 4 year old that you need light in your brain to read! These frameworks of understanding are wonderful to listen to and focus on as an integral part of our planning.

Emotional Intelligence

"The confidence to persevere, to motivate, to believe in oneself and speak out, are all part of the aspect of emotional intelligence." (Goleman D. 1995).

Emotional intelligence helps us to reach our potential through application and perseverance. Our brains can be distracted at any point in the learning process if it is not fully interested and engaged. These engagement points are what I call 'motivational buttons'. We can inspire both children and adults through consultation, offering resources in ways that meet their needs. The more ownership children have the more likely they are to persevere due to intrinsic motivation. The Talking and Thinking Floorbooks™ give an opportunity for children to share their thinking and increase their involvement.

Feedback Loops

The brain thrives on precise feedback. When children are allowed to follow through their own ideas we can follow a path that gives them relevant feedback about things that matter to them. This metacognition is effective when we create links across learning for children, through opportunities like mapping. In the 3D mind maps we start from what they know and then move forward, considering new pieces of information. This process of accepting and rejecting ideas is a critical part of the Talking and Thinking Floorbooks™. We should celebrate the thinking process since it gives children the opportunity to get feedback from each other, from adults and through direct exploration themselves.

Learning strategies

The cognitive psychologists have explored the way that children think and learn. The image that we create a scaffold of known facts and then attach our new knowledge to it has been used for some time in education. They have referred to the process as inductive inference. However the new research suggests that perhaps we try to push children to think in an adult way. Inductive inference can be achieved in two main ways, category-based inference and similarity based inference. The category–based inference pulls information together and makes generalisations about the group in order to assimilate rapidly. Most adults seem to learn in this way until a 'specialist' develops. So we think of trees in a large group and make generalisations that there are deciduous and evergreen trees. In those groups we simplify the fact that 'evergreens are all conifers' and vice versa. In actual fact not all conifers are evergreens. Adults appear to make assumptions that all the objects in the same group share all the same properties. This leads to inaccuracy.

Children however learn through similarity based inference, where observations of similarities and differences lead children to create ideas such as frameworks of understanding. Each time a new piece of information comes along children look closely for similarities and differences. Looking at trees they might create groups based on similarities such as bark that feels a certain way, trees that are by water, that have wobbly leaves, or branches with black buds. This way of looking at the detail of similarities and differences is different to the way that most adults would look at them.

We need to consider the opportunities that children have to think about new information and give them the opportunity to look at similarities and differences of smaller groups. When we consider this in relation to something as everyday as spoons, it begins to clarify why child centred planning is far more effective for learning. The knowledge that each of us holds about spoons is actually phenomenal. No two spoons are ever totally the same; each has its own story, marks, construction, and sound. We can describe them verbally and linguistically in a thousand different ways. Some of us visualise a style or a colour, perhaps even a texture that may have been a memory stored away from our earliest days. The Bag of Discovery has been carefully structured to challenge most of the common statements about spoons, so there are some tasting spoons with two ends, the mustard spoon with no dip, the decorative spoon, and the Scottish spurtle which is used like a spoon to stir.

Multiple Intelligences

Howard Gardner (1983) uses a phrase that says;
"It's not how smart you are that matters, what really counts is " How are you smart?"

The idea that we all have talents and strengths has been around for many years, Howard Gardner has however gone further to suggest that there are 8 intelligences that enable us to consider the way in which we are smart and which 'intelligences we are developing'. Put very simply:

Interpersonal - people who work well in groups or teams

Intrapersonal - people who can work on their own to solve problems, personal targets, self-assessment.

Naturalist - people with a strong natural intelligence interested in any thing to do with nature and the natural world.

Verbal/Linguistic - people who enjoy words and language

Musical/Rhythmic - people with a strong musical intelligence, natural sensitivity to pitch, tone and rhythm

Visual/Spatial - people who are good at thinking in pictures, designs, charts

Bodily kinaesthetic - people who feel confident and able to control their body in sport, dance and drama.

Logical/Mathematical - people who feel positive with numbers and can recognise patterns easily.

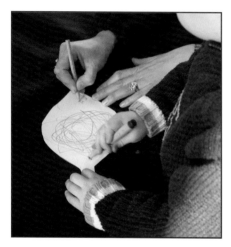 

When we use this approach of Talking and Thinking Floorbooks™ we can;

❖ respond to individual intelligences, through our play based experiences.

❖ enable children to share their own perspectives of a subject that may not have featured in our thinking.

❖ support the emotional development of the children through affirmation, by valuing what they think and offer to us.

❖ understand the need that some children have for varying degrees of structure and order in their play, and the way that we can support them through resources, time, space and adult interaction.

❖ use a methodology that responds to the learning styles, so that the play becomes more closely matched to the needs and desires of the children.

❖ begin to understand the opportunities that will motivate children to challenge themselves through taking on board their ideas and consulting them in the process.

❖ enable the feedback loop of meta-cognition to reach the children so that observation, discussion, recording and planning are in a continuous path that integrates the child as an individual, rather than in a line away from the child towards too much adult direction.

So when all the elements are put together it is apparent that children are engaged in learning in a creative way. This is the stuff of childhood, a place of awe and wonderment that should be celebrated. I promote this process of consultation and planning with children through the Talking and Thinking Floorbooks™. Each book has its own features and style, the core elements are detailed in the following sections.

Talking and Thinking Floorbooks™

What is a Talking & Thinking Book ?

The features of a Talking and Thinking Book include:-

- ***Children's ideas and thoughts*** without re-framing or interpretation so that they are a genuine record of their thinking. When children give a response to a question or contribute an idea that is far removed from the rest of the group thinking, the idea should be recorded as evidence of contribution, but not engagement.

- ***Open ended questions*** that are created in response to an interest from the children. The questions are posed as part of a conversation and are designed to stimulate thought rather than test knowledge. The flow of reflective talk is critical to the process, to create a partnership of exploration and discovery. Question and answer sessions create a completely different atmosphere. Questions are almost philosophical, such as I wonder what would happen if..?

- ***Higher order thinking.*** This level of interest can be stimulated by challenging children to create links in their own learning. Revisiting ideas over long blocks of time support children to see that the process of thinking and learning is full of experimentation and adaptation. The frameworks of understanding that children hold in their brains are created by a wide variety of sensorial input from all the environments they encounter. The Talking and Thinking Books are a method of finding out what they know before, during and after a block of structured experiences.

- ***Depth of Learning.*** The flow of the book follows children's desire to explore an area in depth. Depth of learning created through giving children time to explore their own thinking is the key to long term embedded knowledge. Collating children's ideas in a book form ensures that the group focus on continuity and progression over longer blocks of time. A discussion that starts within the planning aspect of spring, may focus entirely on how plants know to grow, or what is inside a seed. The rate at which some adult-created, disjointed experiences are presented to children can surely only encourage superficial awareness.

- ***Collaborative learning.*** The books include very large pieces of blank paper that enable children and adults to record their ideas as a group. By giving each person a different coloured marker it is possible to observe who contributes to the group writing. The adult provides a role model for the process of thinking, listening, supporting, suggesting ideas, accepting challenge, being a writer, making diagrams, Mind Maps® to name just a few.

- **A variety of methods of presenting thinking.** To respond to different learning styles and preferences the books incorporate a wide range of writing. The adult can scribe for the children to release some from the pressure of secretarial skills during a small group experience; individuals can record their idea in a pictorial form, or writing on a thinking bubble (paper shaped in a thought bubble available freely

in writing area) during the play session; photographs or adult observations are included to show the process of exploration and links between children and their learning: The status given to this creates an atmosphere that celebrates the joy of learning. Children will offer challenging questions and become keen to offer ideas and suggestions that are then incorporated into the planning framework.

- **Collates child centred ideas that are taken forward by the Early Years staff.** Talking and thinking books are an integral part of planning. They are created with children during the play session, and should be used to analyse the starting points for learning that children are suggesting, rather than adults thinking up random 'activities' for children to 'do'. Responsive planning should be at the root of learning. If we are going to consult children then we should be prepared to change our thinking and actions as a result of it. If the children you are working with have limited oracy then the range of strategies should reflect this, increased observation, use of models, or a 3D mind map are all possibilities.

• **The books are available to children at all times.** Joint ownership should give children the right to revisit their thinking whenever they wish. There has to be feedback loop to the children so that they know that the process of consultation is actually changing something. The results of 'meetings' can be recorded, as can voting diagrams and their results. Photographs of physical changes can support this process.

In practice this approach has led to a child centred curriculum, which is based on evidence collated in a child centred way.

- An existing interest will enable children to contribute more effectively
- The ethos of the centre creates the climate for consultation
- The size of the floorbook affects the way children engage with them
- Children should be involved in the process of making the book

A new way of working.

When planning experiences for children the first option staff should consider is the experiences that children bring with them from their home environment. Some possibilities are to consider the interest details that are put onto the transition record such as songs, stories, rhymes, places to go, people at home, or perhaps pets/special friends. These may be familiar themes. However there is a difference in the approach to the experiences and how we consult the children throughout the process. This enables the adults to follow and extend children's thinking rather than creating 'activities' that are presented to children.

'Group writing'

'Giving children acknowledgment by using their name'

Introducing the floorbook to young children for the first time.

It is essential that children feel valued and supported in their environment. Without a positive ethos that demonstrates that children's ideas have value and are important, children are likely to contribute less. To feel that your opinion matters is an internal feeling that is created through the ethos of the centre and subtle nuances of human interaction. People open up their thinking and are more prepared to share their thoughts, if they think they will be listened to and valued. We have to consider the implicit messages we send to children, so that they are clear that we want to hear what they have to say.

Over the years I have seen many types of adult interaction. All of the successful ones involved adults appearing open, interested and motivated by the opinions of children.

The floorbooks share

- Ideas
- Thoughts
- Plans
- Reflections
- Action
- Desires
- Challenges, solutions & failures
- Observations

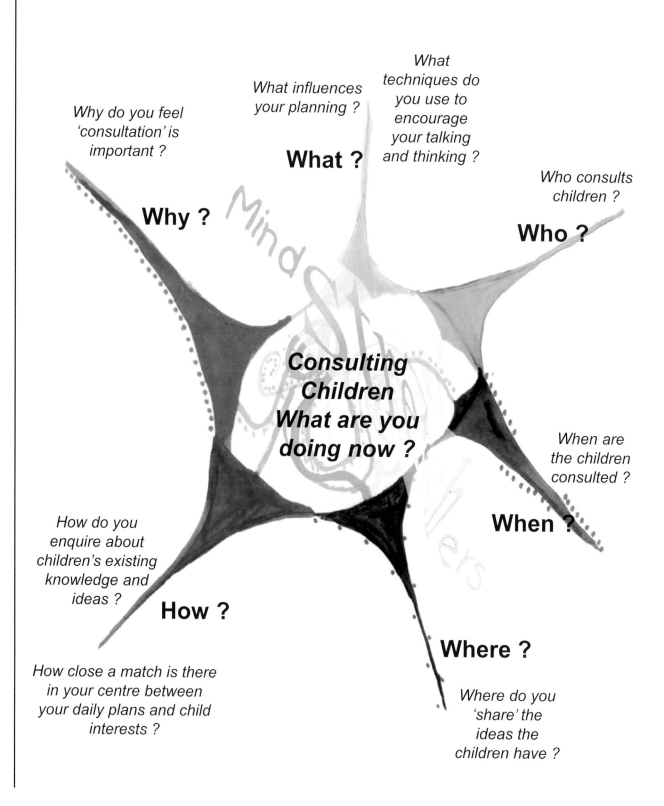

Why do you feel 'consultation' is important ?

What influences your planning ?

What techniques do you use to encourage your talking and thinking ?

What ?

Why ?

Who consults children ?

Who ?

Consulting Children What are you doing now ?

When are the children consulted ?

When ?

How do you enquire about children's existing knowledge and ideas ?

How ?

Where ?

How close a match is there in your centre between your daily plans and child interests ?

Where do you 'share' the ideas the children have ?

Big Floorbooks

The idea of a floorbook came about from childrens love and 'need ' to be kinaesthetic in their learning. Through placing it on the floor it becomes accessible to all the children sitting around it. A circle is a powerful symbol of equality and that is one of the elements of the approach. Children crawl around it, sit by it, and often 'on' it to look in detail at a photograph. As the years move on, and my knees feel the strain, I have started using them at tables with the children free and able to move around ! Some

Kathleen's
Pink Group
Planning Book

centres have started to refer to the approach as big book planning, rather than floorbooks. After many years of working with Talking & Thinking Floorbooks™ I would suggest that it is well worth investing in high quality card and materials. Developing the skill of stitching books in a way that can withstand the constant handling that they will receive, is time well spent.

When I started teaching in Wiltshire I was privileged to be able to work with a gentleman called Ian Bennett. He introduced us to the joyful experience of making books with children. At that stage the children were encouraged to make hardbacked books to display their work. The process and ultimate products were stunning in their creativity. The feeling of ownership was very powerful and could be seen to affect their motivation. As I began to work with much younger children the approach was sustained through simplified techniques. The strength of a book lies in the spine. The stitching and thread are critical to this process which is referred to as a 'Five hole book stitch'.

The thread that you use has to be strong enough to hold the book together. Some possibilities are narrow gift ribbon, nylon wool or bookmakers thread.
The stitching uses five holes, hence the name !!

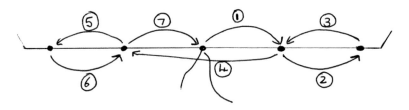

The Process of Making The Book

This process is full of learning. Children enjoy creating the book as much as writing in it. This sequence is adult directed for the development of a skill. It should be complemented by writing zones and bookmaking areas that are full of experimentation, creativity and a wide range of resources so that children can make their own books in any way they wish.

1. Measure out the spine of the book and find the middle point, mark with a dot.
2. Divide the space either side of this mark into 3 and mark the two inner points.
3. Make a hole on each of the dots. Use a sharp pencil onto a soft surface or an awl onto a cork mat. With younger children cut small 'v' shapes on the dots to make it easier to thread the ribbon through.

4. Measure out the ribbon so that it is 3 times the length of the spine. This will ensure that you have enough to complete the stitching and tie it off.
5. When working with older children we use bulldog clips to fasten one end of the ribbon to the edge of the book so that the end of the ribbon remains in place and doesn't get pulled through.
6. It can help children to use pegs to hold the pages together or they can use a friend's hands !!
A five hole book stitch holds the pages firmly and can be undone if more pages need to be included.

Children are the authors of the book and therefore sign their names at the start and usually design and make the cover boards. It is important for each group to identify their book as being unique and individual.

Writing on thinking bubbles

Include large A4 envelopes so that children who want to make tiny books and store them in the big book can do so. Place a photo on the outside and name to aid recognition. Once the methodology is set, I place the actual book on the floor. Although dimensions are not too critical, being 'involved' in a giant book does hold an attraction. Ownership of the book is paramount, so it is recommended that children design the cover in any way they wish. Some of the covers are fabric, others card, some remain as rough paper.

Sample Covers

- Children should see the effect their ideas have through our planning.
- Talking and Thinking Floorbooks™ can be used in a variety of ways to support the needs of children.
- Child initiated ideas often focus on details within a larger interest.
- Child initiated interests last for a range of durations, depending on motivation.

Where does the starting point come from ?
Child initiated experiences

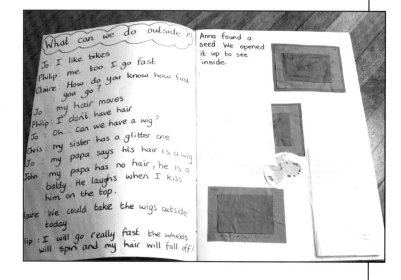

Many people may take observations and then talk about them at planning meetings without the children being aware of it. Do the children see the way that their ideas are taken into account ? Do they see how their ideas influence day to day experiences in the nursery ? The feedback loop is important for all people, especially children. Any observations made by the staff should flow over a number of sessions before they influence the whole provision. Children often have a cursory interest in a subject, as well as more widespread ideas. If the floorbook followed each idea, provision would become too fragmented. There will be common links and ideas that integrate and flow through children's play.

In large nurseries the method of transfer of observations is critical to their effectiveness.

- Some staff use a Talking and Thinking Floorbook™ in each room and take the children's thinking to the planning meeting. This enables staff to use observations made by adults, tracking records and deeper thinking and engagement to influence the planning.

- In smaller centres talking and thinking books have been linked to areas of play such as the role play zone.

- In others each key group has a book and they record thinking at any point in the play session, but also through structured consultation times with an adult.

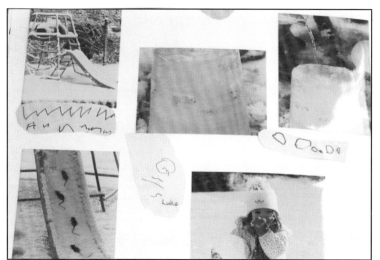

Children should be able to record thinking without correction & adult writing

- The other option would be to explore a shared interest across the nursery which may flow from room to room and group to group.

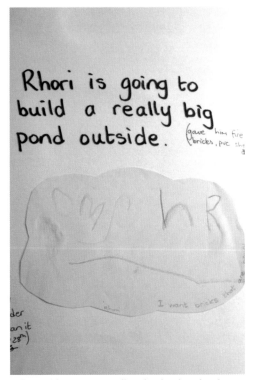

Practitioner recording in the book when they have responded to a child's interest

The group that write in the book can therefore be grouped socially, intellectually, or emotionally through shared motivation or need. Within this, the group can therefore be self selected or gathered by the adults.

The strength of the approach lies in the flexibility it has to children's interests so it may occur that the umbrella interest is water, but the red group are following rain and within that there are two individuals who want to explore puddles and record their ideas in their own small books held in larger envelopes within the more generic Talking and Thinking Floorbook™.

The starting point that I like to start with is often totally child initiated. The evidence to support this comes from observations and conversations that are made throughout the nursery. Insights can often be gained at the snack table by listening to children to find out threads of interest. The subjects that inspire children are often connected directly to the human side of life. When we talk about people who help us,the focus that the children have is, What police people eat for breakfast and what would happen if they lost the keys to the handcuffs

There is enough scope for early years practitioners to take up any one of the interests highlighted above, such as the handcuffs and explore what they should be made of. How many different types of keys there are ? How many different locks ? These questions can lead to the creation of technology and science based Talking and Thinking Floorbooks™ with the children.
So the idea of people who help us has gone down to an investigation intohandcuffs. The learning and understanding is in fact larger because children will explore, handcuffs with combination locks, handcuffs for giants, mechanisms, catches, materials and their properties.

Kara's spider is a wee, wee spider and it is beside the Daddy spider.
It has two parts to its body and two codes. (Kara pointed to the feelers).

Child drawing supported by a photograph of the process of play

Case study for child initiated experiences

The Little House

Iain and Iona were working in the woodwork corner and decided to make a bedroom for the Little Folk. They used an empty toolbox as the room and Iona made a table with

 chairs attached to it so they "could all have their tea sitting close" while Iain made a little bed out of cardboard. Iona made a chair with foam cushions so "they have warm bottoms". Iain decided to make a 'magic playground with roller-skates (polystyrene shapes) and flowers (snowdrops).

The chimney developed "I can balance it", "we need wool", "tiny bit", "that is too long", we need shorter, this height",

 "attach this, tie the chimney on", "Iona can you hold this to me as I fix the chimney", "that's good Iain", "we need more string", "did you forget to hold it Iona" "you tie it Melissa, you can be a good 'tier'"

Iona decides the lid of the Smartie box would make a good plate. They filled it with broken matches to make food. "bit much food, they get fat" "We can use matches as spoons, actually too spiky on their mouths, could make them sick, spiky in their tummies"

At this stage I asked if they would like a bigger box and after some discussion this was enthusiastically accepted "We need to decorate for a boy and a girl" "we need to make a

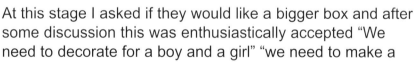 clock" so Iain cut some orange paper and wrote numbers on. "A person picture for them to do another one". " we need toys".

 Calum joined them. "this could be a windmill" – nailing the polystyrene shape to the wall. "This is going to be a tortoise" "a toy one?", "no a real one, no a pretend one" James joined in "I'll make a trampoline", "are you telling me you're making ANOTHER windmill?"

Iain wanted to fill the red box with toys for them
"an aeroplane", " no, also good toys for girls Iain"

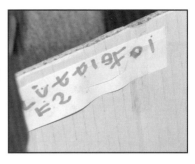

James "I'm going to number the door – number 8 …and some letters too"

Kennedy " I need to tidy the house, it's a terrible mess'

Keziah suggested they make their own house "our house needs a roof and door", "let's make a handle so we can open the door", "I need an old towel", "what for?" "the carpet"

Keziah " I need some sellotape – I need to make paper hats for the Little Folk.

Iain - "I think I need a box, to make a study"
"we also need a garage" " here is the car",
"it's not a real car, just pretend"
"We need a ramp so they can get in"

This spontaneous activity developed over four days and involved many of the children although initiated by Iona and Iain. The talking & thinking, lists of materials requested, childrens plans, the photographs of process and the adult planning sheet were included in the Talking & Thinking Floorbook™.

- Adults can initiate/influence play in positive ways.
- The pace of play and structured opportunities influence depth of learning.

Where does the starting point come from ?
Adult initiated experiences

The planning process should be a blend of child and staff weaving a framework of opportunities together. With every best will in the world it would be impossible to create a match between provision and need for every child all the time. What we do need to do is create a better match that is informed so that the halves come together with understanding and insight.

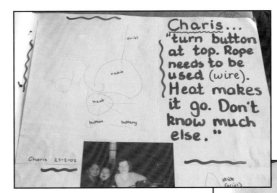

Adult initiated activity to introduce exploration of technology

There will be points in the play experience when the adult makes decisions based on need, balance of the curriculum, or perhaps gender imbalance. In this instance the adult was very aware of the 'motivational buttons' of the children and had an insight into the aspects of a subject that they would really enjoy. This awareness of learning styles and hemisphere dominance cuts across curricular subjects and allows us to focus on methodology that can aid us in the delivery of an idea.

However some ideas bear little relation or connection to the children around them. I saw seven balloons covered in paper mache hanging from the roof of a centre, each one painted a different colour. When I asked a child if he could tell me something about how they made them, he was animated. Lots of glue, mixture in his hair and on his 'new shoes' showed me that he had been deeply engaged. Then his face changed and he said…'Then they got painted and now we can't touch them, up there' when I looked at the planning framework the balloons had taken over a week to make, and the main idea behind the activity was to 'teach the solar system'. I know that some children may find space engaging, but it is highly unlikely that any child would suggest daily layering of mache, then a week's drying and then elevation. What did inspire that young child was the making of the paper mache, and then the challenge of it dropping off the balloon.

In terms of adult initiated experiences I have seen posters arrive asking for new astronauts, large pieces of white and silver fabric arrive in response to an urgent request from the children to create a rocket. Lunches have been packed and the play has been fresh but based on the learning and interest.

The rate of change.

In order to 'move through' the curriculum it would appear that practitioners often feel compelled to initiate more opportunities than are really necessary. It would appear that when under pressure some staff feel that it is more effective that the 'pace of change ' is fast. Unfortunately I do not believe that deep learning (the kind that stays with you) can be achieved at this rate. Do children want to look at all of the 'people who help us' or perhaps one or two and really get to know them, even down to what they have in their 'packed lunch'.

When I visit centres it does fascinate me when I interact with children to hear their perception of what we are doing. I was in a nursery at the time of Burns night. When a little boy came dancing across in his kilt, as he passed me he said ' See me. I'm gonna be a Chinese singer like Rabbie!' The passage of time between Chinese New Year and Burns night was obviously so close that he felt they were all about the same thing!

Adult initiated activity to stimulate thinking

There are centres that have created a wonderful blend of adult initiation and child interaction. In response to an adult initiated Talking Tub™ on food, children showed a clear desire to explore potatoes.

They wanted to sort them out into 'little holes' so the adult sourced black potatoes, white, dark brown and sweet potatoes.

They wanted to know which bit grew so they left them on the window sill to 'chit'.

Some children wanted to dig so the adults put the potatoes in the materials tray with potting compost.

Cooking potatoes took over the snack area and children were offered the opportunity to cook 'microwave crisps', mashed and boiled potatoes. Without the adult to initiate and extend the play the children may never have had the opportunity to experience a wide and balanced curriculum.

Professor Tony Pellegrini refers to high adult direction where resources, time, space and focus are dictated by the adult as non-play. He refers to completely child initiated play as pure play since time, space, resources and focus are all denoted by the child. By

Adult initiated activity on planting seeds

virtue of the fact that children enter some structure by attending our early years environments the point we want to achieve is halfway along a continuum between the two.

Case study adult initiated experiences

Bird Hide

It was apparent from our overview that the children had limited experiences with design and technology. Knowing that a lot of children in the nursery loved 'bird watching' they were asked if they would like to build one. It was quite basic at first, but the children added their own ideas. Fraser G. thought a camouflage net was needed in case the birds saw them looking. Some of the children put up drawings inside the hide to make it look better.

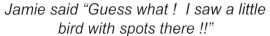
Jamie said "Guess what ! I saw a little bird with spots there !!"

'Look at that one hanging on !'

Fraser said "Get the binoculars - we need to look for different birds"

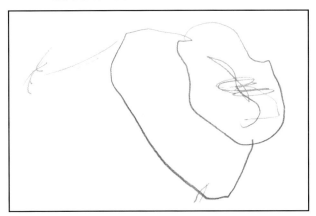

Jamie A. spying through the hide at a bird

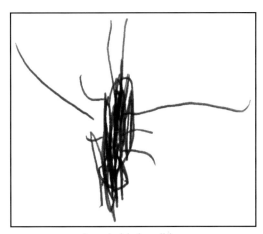

Iona's bird walking

One of the boys pointing out the birds

Jamie said "I need the wee whistley thing so that we can call the birds "

Fraser said "I hope I don't see a crow. They chase the small birdies away and eat their food"

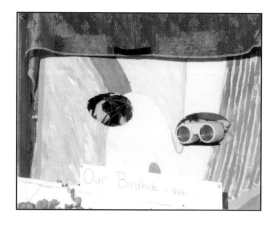

When asked what other animals would try to eat birds other than cats, Fraser said "Crocodiles !"
No they don't replied Marcus, the birds pick things off the crocodile's teeth. I have a book about them."

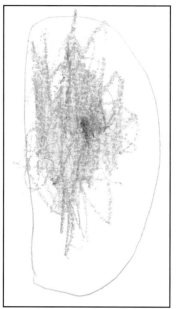

'Bird hiding in the tree, from the cat.'

"They have all gone away. There is a cat. Does the cat eat them ? Shoo shoo - get away"

Fraser sent Jamie to ask me to chase away the cat !!

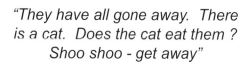

A wide variety of children have visited and enjoyed the hide. Especially Fraser and Jamie, as it was a good way for them to have a 'quiet time'. Even our visiting older children have spent time in the hide.

Ideas and drawings were put in the Talking and Thinking Floorbook™ to show the development of the children's thinking.

- The ethos of the environment is very influential on children's confidence to consult.
- Practitioners need to be skilled communicators, able to question in open-ended ways.
- Children respond well when they can make informed choices.
- Children communicate in a variety of ways.

Effective Questioning

Inappropriate questioning often leads to the shrugging of shoulders, or to a look of uncertainty which is not part of the approach. Children are given time to think and contribute, but not put into a situation that causes stress or discomfort through torture by a thousand questions!
Some questions are inappropriate and confuse or frustrate children.
'What do you want to learn about ? is too complex and children do not know what options there are to choose from.

Questions should encourage children to think & reflect

'What do you want to play ?' often leads to children selecting an area of the nursery, rather than an aspect of learning, or perhaps something not immediately visible in the environment.

At the beginning of the process, adult questions should use reflective, open ended questions that have no set answer, so that children offer a great variety of thoughts and ideas. When the initial general focus has come from children then the adult follows the idea that either

- has most support and interest

or

- one that can offer the experiences she/he feels that the children need at that point in their learning.

The questions are usually phrased.. How do you think..? What do you feel might..? Where will you..? When will you...? How can we help ? What do you need ?

These questions enable staff to create a complete picture of what the children know, what they are interested in, and how they want to take it forward. This information is essential if the play is to develop in a way that is appropriate to their understanding.

Choices
To support choices, children need to have information within their experiences. If the experiences are on the edge of their knowledge the practitioner will need to support their choices.
Some options are outlined in this book. Any of these strategies can be used at a variety of times.

The greatest influence on the effectiveness of a centre is one of the most intangible. The ethos. The feeling you get when you walk into a centre tells you a great deal about the way that the staff and children work together.

I was recently delivering a course on citizenship and I was interested to note the way that adult groups are able to put forward models and diagrams with all the right words, but their behaviours during the day gave a different message. When people found it difficult to speak, or where there were people who spoke too much, their responses were irritation. When spelling was an issue someone tutted. People spoke, and people didn't look at them to show interest. Adults need to practice what they preach.

This approach is based on mutual respect and a desire to listen and respond. Children will pick the 'real meaning' from the way that adults talk to each other, by the way that they are spoken to and treated. The adult role is therefore crucial to the effectiveness of this way of working.

Children will tell you what they think if they;

- feel valued
- are given time
- know that you will accept their thinking without judgement
- can communicate in the best way for them
- can tell you when they feel the time is right
- know that you are really interested
- see you looking at them
- know that you are listening to them
- see their ideas/suggestions actually being used.
- know something about the subject you are questioning them about!

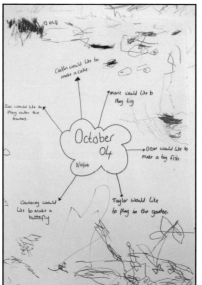

2D mind map

Children will communicate with you about experiences, objects, and feelings. The way that they do that will vary with every child.

- Some children point and gesture.
- Some move symbols and pictures.
- Some are vocal and use their language.
- Some use their whole body to show what they think.

As a culture perhaps we need to be able to develop the skill of reading body language rather than relying on questioning.

- **3D objects stimulate the senses and therefore 'switch' on the brain.**
- **Related objects can be used to create connections in learning.**
- **2D images can show the potential of an area/possibilities of play for adults and children.**

A Talking Tub™ is a collection of materials that are designed to stimulate talking and thinking. Many children need a stimulus to start the process of thinking. The Talking Tub™ offers a range of materials that stimulate observation and discussion. It can be created in response to the interest in a key group or as a general tub for use across the whole nursery. The advantage of the Talking Tub™ being created by the key worker is that they can respond more effectively to individual interests.

The way that the box is presented is important to the overall image of the experience. Our box has question marks all over it, we have used decorated cardboard boxes, or perhaps a wooden chest with feathers glued on. The important message to include is that the things in the box are for thinking about, that there is no right answer.

3D objects.

The objects are designed to be three dimensional so that they stimulate all the senses. Children can interact with them and stimulate their brains in the process. For example in a Talking Tub™ about people who help us, the objects tend to show the human aspect of people who help us rather than an outward appearance.

The fire brigade box may include a piece of blue fabric that is strong/fireproof, a walkie talkie, a timetable to know when they are on shifts, a cover for eyes to allow them to sleep. The objects that you put into the Talking Tub™ should not be too obvious. The aim is to stimulate the brain to think, rather than merely identify and name the objects. The fabric in this tub could take the conversation into flame retardancy, colour, texture or use. The walkie talkie could lead to discussions about radio reception, controls, volume, use of batteries, recharging and codes of communication. The timetable offers children the chance to talk about people they know that work on a shift rota. This could take the conversation around to talking about police, fire, hospital staff, factory workers, bakers etc. The fact that children can make connections between the discussion in the centre and their lives outside will enable them to retain the information more effectively.

Thinking about plants

Examples from practice

The Vets
A dog tag and code number may develop into an interest in number cataloguing. Empty flea shampoo bottle and flea comb could lead to discussions around care. A range of appointment cards supports children in their comparison of going to the health centre

with the vets. Head collars for a range of animals, such as rabbit harnesses, ferret lead and cat collars stimulate wonderful talk about the challenge of exercising any animal. There is no reason why a three year old cannot take a spider for a walk !

Christian Nativity
Straw and hay could lead to discussions about mattresses, sleeping areas and smell. Blue cloth and hessian may lead to the creation of plant dyes, texture or weaving. Baby hospital band and a baby bottle may lead to comparative talk about the range of maternity conditions between then and now. Many children have some awareness of babies, so that much of their knowledge will be based on practical aspects such as nappy changing, feeding or prams.

Three dimensional objects encourage children to engage in a sensorial way. The tub can be used at any point to stimulate discussion or raise awareness.
Children are stimulated through the experience of handling materials but then, all of us are. Our brains are able to handle an object and think. In fact the stimulation may well bring forward ideas - so why then do we ask our children to sit still, not fiddle and think ?

One way of using the Talking Tub™ is to create linked 3D objects in response to group interest. If the umbrella is 'Animals', it is possible to focus on elements within that, such as fish, dogs and rabbits. The resources in the Talking Tub™ alter with each group, whilst the underpinning concepts or knowledge awareness are the same, such as care routine, food or skin texture. Most centres have displays that celebrate a range of animals, the vets can be meaningful for any focus, so the depth of learning comes through group interest.

The Talking Tub™ materials can be used in the 3D mind maps to stimulate discussion in a more adult directed way. The photograph opposite shows a Talking Tub™ based on water. This box includes a variety of objects such as bottles, a flannel, a plug and a toothbrush.

Collection of water-based objects

Some elements may have been on a display - but the key is surely that ....

'It ain't what you do it's the way that you do it,
that's what gets results' - Bananarama

Consultation, interaction, handling resources and engagement are all key to a dynamic play environment.

2D objects

The 2D photographs will work to give children visual cues for the possibilities of play.

For example an area that is currently being developed is the outdoor area. Children need to be involved in the process of choosing opportunities but unless you have the seed of a vision it can be very hard to come up with unique experiences.

A group of children created a letterbox from a tulip, a den from some sticks, petal perfume and wonderful constructions from crates and guttering. With a vision in their heads children use these ideas as stepping stones for further play. Without a pebble to start a ripple, some ideas may never appear.

Many children are visual learners, and so 2D photographs are an easy way of recording an event or showing some possibilities. Many centres have now built up a comprehensive stock of photographs that record play. The photographs can actually show a variety of messages and so we need to consider the content of the ones we use. The better the photograph the more potential it has for quality talking and thinking.

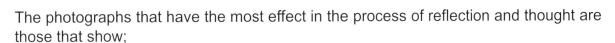

The photographs that have the most effect in the process of reflection and thought are those that show;

~ Children deeply involved in play rather than posed smiles. Children respond to emotion, they comment by saying things like 'That boy is really having to try' 'Why can't that girl do it?' 'It's good that he reached up to that, I'd use a big ladder because I am not as tall as him' 'That must be really good eh? Bit hard, but cool anyway'

~ Children in a series of sequence shots. When we are trying to show perseverance with task it can be difficult to show the passage of time. Sequence shots can give the same sense of achievement as we feel when we read 'before and after' stories in adult magazines. Photographs can show the change and the effort required, which has given rise to the following types of comment. " I done that!" " "He spent all the time on that tower, it must be ages" "Did her mum help?"

~ Ways of playing that have not been experienced within the setting. Although play is totally natural to most children there are some opportunities that can be started by dropping a pebble into the pool. They give a view that is different, the way is not copied to the point of detail, but does offer an initial idea. The photographs may look at an area of play, or the types of play happening in the space. An example would be in the use of the guttering outside. One resource, but used in a thousand different ways.

~ Detail. Children learn from each other, as well as from themselves, adults, and the environment. Photograph the lashings and knots used on a den building site. The photographs can be put into an album and used as part of the group discussion about dens and structures and how to make them safe.

~ Landscape and resources. Sand pits seem to be simple, but when you show children the potential of the way that it can be presented, both inside and out, putting it in a rectangular tray seems very plain. Consider photographs of square sand pits, a sand wall (trough on top of low wall), sand pits that include frames and plants, sand pits that are in a tiny container with tiny objects, sand under the Perspex floor, sand areas in a spiral, sand in barrels spread across an area, sand tray in the role play area to use for pretend cooking or sand on a large mat to sit in inside.

The photographs can be presented in a variety of ways. The P.L.O.D.S (Possible Line of Development) we use are coded so that we can select those that are linked to;
• a curricular area such as mathematics or science.
• an issue such as gender bias.
• demonstrating a skill or attitude.
• a piece of knowledge such as a specific bird or the shape of a snail.
• holistic or seasonal opportunities.

The selection of photographs enables the adult to stimulate talk and ideas within the group of children, whilst focusing on the subject. An example might be an observation that has led to noting that some boys are saying that the "dolls are girlie". To challenge this statement the practitioner has several choices. One is to say "No !" Another is to talk through the issue and raise awareness. By presenting a photograph such as the one on the right, the adult can encourage children to talk about what they see and how they feel about it.

Strong visual images

To create a visual space and to aid visual perception I use a large black Talkaround Mat™. The photos are spread all over it or just around the edge and children can move around to see a photo they like. Sometimes I might give a child a photo because it links to their personal interest for example Chris loves spiders, so the web covered in dew goes near him.

3 Dimensional mind mapping

- **3D mind mapping is a strategy that enables children to make connections and create ideas.**
- **Preparation makes effective use of short blocks of consultation time.**
- **Evidence is gathered through photography since the process is transient.**

Mind Maps® have been written about by Tony Buzan for some time now to show the links in learning. They are used effectively to enable people to make connections between pieces of knowledge and ideas, because they support whole brain learning, they are now widely used in schools. For younger children, the 2D mind map can be recorded by the adult to demonstrate the way that ideas connect. The 3D mind map is more effective in my practice because it is kinaesthetic and sensorial.

Preparation is always the key to being responsive! My preparation includes gathering these resources; Talkaround Mat™ to create a visual space to work on.
Bubble shaped thinking paper
Marker pens for adult and child

Stimulation through sensorial experiences

Central object to focus attention

Strips of paper or ribbon
Objects that link to the subject that interests the children, so if the children are exploring light it might be a range of torches such as dynamo, electromagnetic, wind up, batteries or different types, old torch and screwdrivers, photographs of sunshine and darkness, sunglasses, suncream, hat, reflective strips and so on.

Mind mapping when we use it, follows a sequence that incorporates the following elements. Although, as all early years practitioners know, children often invent their own unique way of doing things.

Stimulus

A resource is placed in the centre to focus on, the real ones are the most engaging which is possible if it is water or hats, slightly more challenging when it is crocodiles!

Sharing knowledge

From this, children talk about what they think or want to know about. When they suggest an idea

Children recording their ideas

that can be represented by an object they place it on the map, if the idea is abstract it can be recorded on the bubble paper and placed anywhere on the map. At the end of their interest and celebrate their achievement.

The Adult Role

The affirmation that children receive from the active listening strategies of eye contact, body language and facial expression all affect the way the child feels about themselves as a thinker. The adult role at this point is to decode and listen to ideas without alteration. Some children may need further open-ended questions to enable them to share what they know.

Positive adult interaction

Simple structure along pathways.

The simplest steps to creating a linking mind map are to sort ideas along pathways. Place the 3D object in the middle. Radiate out lines of ribbon/paper. Use the children's thinking bubbles. Read out the idea and then ask children where it should go.
An example linked to water might be pathways such as bathtime, drinking, playing, the weather.
Along the bathtime pathway you might have a rubber duck, shampoo bottle, flannel.
Along the drinking pathway it might be a cup, a straw, a teabag.
Along the playing pathway it might be water balloons, a water pistol (or photo!), a bucket, Wellington boots
Along the weather pathway it might be a photo of a cloud, an umbrella or a puddle.

Reflecting Understanding

Thinking about how ideas are connected

If the child puts the idea on an unconnected pathway accept it. This is reflective of their understanding, not the correct answer. Many children will correct each other in a more severe way than adults would use. The adult needs to be there to facilitate the situation and model an appropriate way of saying that opinions do vary. The adult should consider when to interact to challenge the idea put forward. It may be a casual use of the related words during a play session, or a structured opportunity at group time, or a focused opportunity offered through the play room.

Creating connections

Most connected objects should be in the resource box or in the nursery. Children put the 3D objects down and then the adult or child places a ribbon to connect the two. At this point it may be enough to celebrate that the group have made connections and links and leave it at that. An example might be that a flannel, a sponge and a bar of soap are all used at bath time.

Next steps

Through re-visiting their thinking the adult can challenge them to talk about the connections in their ideas to make a more cohesive map.
When children are familiar with the idea, the connections can be written on the strip of paper.
E.g. Night time picture - we need a - torch -needs- battery - no battery - dynamo torch.
Although children will not decode the writing they will make a connection between the written and the spoken word. They will also identify which piece of writing is their own.

3D mind map

Recording the Evidence

To the untrained eye the mind map can look random. In actual fact the process of considering each idea and how it links to something else is simple and repetitive. The connections and lines make sense to the people involved in it.
The process of recording the 3D map can start at any point. Photographs that show the build up show the process of thinking; photographs of previous maps can encourage reflection; photographs or diagrams of the whole map can show achievement. The product is transient and for many children they enjoy the movable nature of the map. It can be adjusted and re-made as many times as they like.

Challenge and problem solving

It can be effective to keep the objects as part of their Talking Tub™, and use them to re-visit the thinking and learning on an ongoing basis. Through deeper discussions and handling of 3D objects, children will often come upon a problem that they feel they want to investigate. For example in the winter a child had slipped on some ice when they were at home. When she came to the Talking Tub™ on water she picked out the wellington boots and started to tell us about the sole of the boot and how it didn't work on ice. This in turn lead to an investigation into 'what makes things slippy'.
The problems that children want to investigate will be about the smaller scale issues that affect their daily lives.

Progression

In order for children to progress we need to offer them time to mature and stimulating opportunities to encourage them to think. Children move through a 'spiral of learning' that is a balance of child initiated play, adult observation, structured interaction through adult initiated opportunities and epistemic play to explore the potential of new situations and materials. The first Talking Tub™ may be on a general theme of water, through this children show their interest in footwear. The next Talking Tub™ would focus on that, from this discussion children may look at water-proofing. The following Talking Tub™ may contain water-proof fabrics, non water-proof materials, objects that will sprinkle water so that they can investigate water beading, being absorbed etc. This may in turn lead to den building and roofing materials. The pathway is directed by child interest, the adult skill is to understand the concepts and how to extend the learning.

Mindstretchers 3D mind mapping

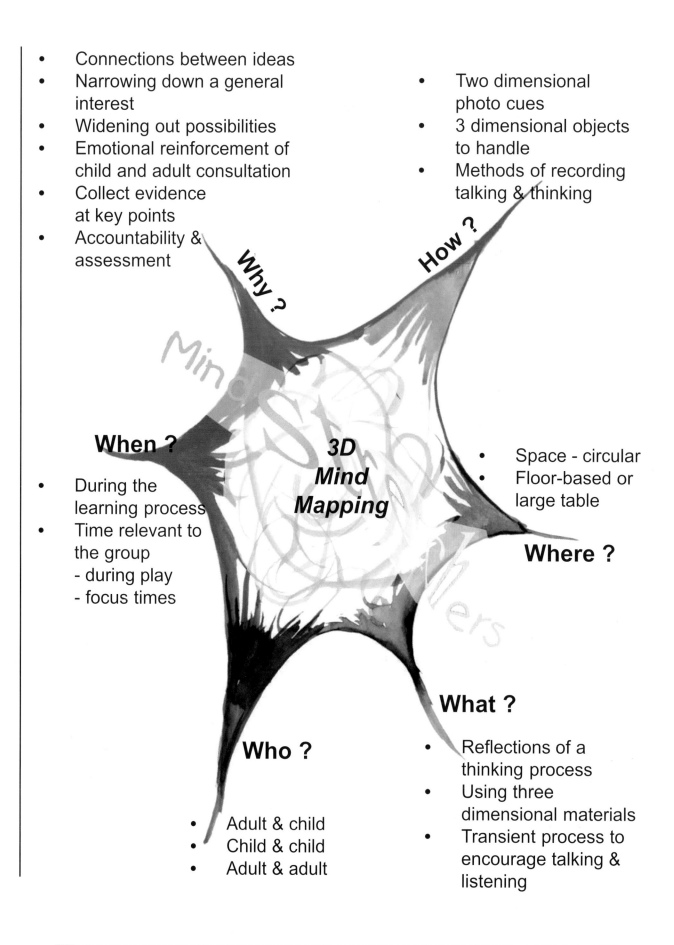

- Connections between ideas
- Narrowing down a general interest
- Widening out possibilities
- Emotional reinforcement of child and adult consultation
- Collect evidence at key points
- Accountability & assessment

Why ?

How ?

- Two dimensional photo cues
- 3 dimensional objects to handle
- Methods of recording talking & thinking

When ?

- During the learning process
- Time relevant to the group
  - during play
  - focus times

3D Mind Mapping

- Space - circular
- Floor-based or large table

Where ?

What ?

- Reflections of a thinking process
- Using three dimensional materials
- Transient process to encourage talking & listening

Who ?

- Adult & child
- Child & child
- Adult & adult

Water

The children in the nursery were interested in playing in the puddles outside. It was decided to focus on water as a possible context for planning.

The black Talkaround Mat™ was laid out in a quieter corner of the nursery. Children self selected to come and join the group.

The bottle of water was put into the middle so that the stimulus was simple at the start. The question was asked " Does anyone know anything that we use water for? At that

point the children's ideas were written up on yellow strips of paper. The child's name was put at the end and a symbol to aid the decoding process. Children said
"Bath with my sister"
" I like splashing"…gestures
"Drink it"
"I want to shake it"
"Brush your teeth"
 The ideas are recorded by the adult on strips of yellow paper, to release the child from the writing process which often allows them to think. There are other points in the strategy for children to record themselves.

At this point another adult came into the group. There are often silent times that are full of thinking, children need this space, but adults often feel the need to say or do something in the gap. The adult decided to share a story of how one day she was having a bath and the phone rang, then she was in the bath talking on the phone. This caused a huge amount of enjoyment and the children wanted to know who she was speaking to, how long for?, What was your phone like? The focus on the water element had gone and the drawings that came from the experience showed the adult in the bath on the telephone as well having a big bath, lots of hot water and a rubber duck! At this point the session stopped and in light of the comments made by the children I made sure that there was a rubber duck in the Talking Tub™ and something to represent a bath.

In the next session a similar group of children came to the Talkaround™ mat. In the Talking Tub™ on water we had bubble bath with a screw top, hand wash pump action nozzle, washing up liquid with a flip nozzle, plug, rubber duck, flannel, swim suit, goggles, swim ticket, rubber arm bands, toothbrush, wellington boots, umbrella, cup and washing tablets. All the elements were put together to stimulate a wide range of interest and many possible lines of development. As the children were handling the materials, the adult noted some of the comments such as

" I like swimming we go with my papa"
"When my mum washes my hair she puts bubbles on top of my head"
"I splash in my bath"
"My mum makes the water hot in the kettle, I can't touch it 'cos its burny"

Possible lines of development

As the bubble paper is starting to fill up, they are spread out over the Talkaround Mat™, to celebrate the amount the children are thinking. As an adult it is possible to monitor who has spoken or shown their ideas in some way. At any point there are often statements such as 'Kelly is thinking hard', 'Philip is enjoying holding the flannel'. This strategy ensures that all children contribute through action, word or gesture.

At another session it would be possible to combine the yellow strips of paper and the thinking bubbles to monitor the interest in the bigger group. By using the thinking bubbles it is possible to sort them out along the lines of interest. The line that holds the most would indicate that is the area that children have some existing knowledge about. This is the place to start planning from. By taking the area of strength, children will be able to give you more ideas and probably have more to contribute to the planning.

The next session can refine and focus the experience into possibilities for activity. If most of the interest is on the bath, I would put a model of a bath or a photograph in the centre of the mat and this time ask the question of 'What shall we find out about baths?" or a more leading question would be "If we were going to change the role play area into a bathroom what would we put in it?. It is these ideas that feed into the planning framework. There may be individual interests identified or their ideas may be part of a general provision.

The paper bubbles are sometimes used for display alongside the drawings and plans the children have made, or they go into a Talking and Thinking Floorbook™ for future reference. Photographs are included to show the process of play.

The discussion during the session impacts on the children's investigation during the free-flow play. The children in these photographs walked around the nursery trying to find where 'the water was hiding' These photographs would be included in the floorbook to show the way that children have extended their exploration through play.

- **Children can use a collaborative talking at a meeting to discuss issues that bother them.**
- **Spaces inside and out can support children to gather together to talk & communicate.**
- **Minutes of a meeting can be kept as a record of consultation.**
- **Children can find their own solutions to most problems.**

'No problem can withstand the assault of sustained thinking' Voltaire

When we work together it enables us to draw on the thinking skills of everyone in that group. The Talking and Thinking Floorbooks™ belong to the community of learning and, therefore, they are located in the book area. All the children have access to them to share their thinking and re-visit their ideas and those of other children. Many children will go back to the book when they face a challenge, for example ' I remember Darren had that pull thing when he made a ship'. The children then went to the book to look at photographs that had been taken. They solved their own problem.

Children are encouraged to write down their ideas and put them into the book, at any point in the play session. We use bubble shaped paper to make it visually different to the writing area paper. Use squared paper/bullet points/lines to give children the choice of layout. Adults can model this skill, by following the same path. Children will imitate adults and if the ability to look back is seen to be positive they will continue this approach across all areas of their learning.

Children as writers

Children are encouraged to call for a meeting if they feel that there are issues they want to share. At the beginning of the process the meetings will be a group time and are often structured by the adult. As the approach becomes embedded in practice it is lovely to see children gathered together with no adult having a meeting to discuss ideas.

The 'minutes' of the meeting can be written up by the adult or as part of the play session with the children. The minutes can then be stuck into the floorbooks to record the ideas. In the photograph shown, the children were having a meeting to discuss the use of a willow tree that had recently been made available to them in their outside area.

Children in a meeting

To stimulate discussion with children they were shown a video by David Attenborough. This gave the children a greater awareness of the potential of natural environments for play. With this increased knowledge they were then able to have meaningful conversations. The adult facilitated the group allowing all children to contribute to the meeting. Some of the children's comments were recorded. Here are a few of their comments

' I like the train.'

'My exciting thing was the bars that you swing on like a monkey.'

'I liked the wee pond'

'Could we have a maze in the nursery ?'

If meetings and forums are to be encouraged as part of the general citizenship of the centre, layout and design should be considered so there are spaces to gather children together both inside and out. There are a variety of ways to support this.

Children identify key activities with routine and visual cues. One of the strategies I use is the

Minutes of a meeting

creation of a mat. The mat is kept in a basket in the gathering area and is put out by the children when we are going to have group discussions. My storytelling mat is a very colourful patchwork quilt, however when I started using this for group discussion it became apparent that the quilt distracted some of the children. At this point I started to use a plain black mat. This focused children on the objects we were handling and the discussion in the group. The circular shape creates a feeling of equality and is used across many emotional, personal and social development programmes. The diameter of the mat I currently use is large enough to seat approximately ten children and an adult around the outside of the mat. This group size is the most appropriate for discussion, large enough to stimulate a range of views, but small enough to engage all the children.

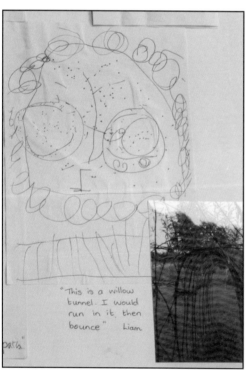

Drawings & diagrams to plan an experience with willow

The outdoor space offers a greater challenge due to the weather. In order to replicate the methodology inside various resources can be used. Children will need a form of shelter such as a small tipi. A place to sit such as the Talkaround Mat™ which is round and waterproof for sessions outside, wooden stumps in a circle, logs on the side. The most important element is a supportive and motivated adult.

Case study for meetings & group discussions

Group discussions happen at any point in the day. They can be adult initiated at a focus time, naturally occurring and then extended through adult interaction, or used as observation to affect the opportunities in the centre.

When children feel empowered and have a sense that their opinions are being valued they will enjoy the idea of 'a meeting'. The concept of being able to call a meeting was brought home to me in a nursery where I was working, when one child who was working in the construction area, said in a loud voice, "That's it! We need a meeting!" at which

'Loading bay for the vehicles'

point they went to an adult who suggested they talk in the quiet area. The practitioner followed them over to provide paper for 'the note taker' and suggest that they get the round mat out. The child who had called the meeting stated very clearly at the start "I can't find the little bricks because everyone keeps putting them in the big bricks". One of the children suggested that they use the blue box for the little bricks, another wanted a basket, and someone else suggested the big green potting tray since it had all little 'bits' in it. The adult supported children by modelling the way that you behave if you are listening, she commented on the way that the 'note taker' was using her book, and then limited their decision making to two options; - to make a container that would sort out the bricks or to find the little bricks. The boy who had called the meeting chose to go and create a brick tub along with several of the children. The others started to look for little bricks and collect them in basket. The group that were making the tub used a biscuit tin and pieces of cardboard to divide the space into seven areas. They used masking tape to fix the cardboard to the sides. The box was then put into the construction area and used by the children to sort the miniature bricks.

Meetings are about group decisions, they model complex behaviours and demonstrate aspects of citizenship such as respecting each other's views, negotiation, compromise and develop solution based approaches rather then problem focused behaviours.

Children have different priorities in their lives and will call meetings about the colour of the water, or behaviour they don't like, or even the number of bits of tomato they can have at snack. These are the things that are important to them, so we should acknowledge this. One way of doing it is to listen and respond. Just as adults, some children will call meetings to attract attention. If there are other channels for their ideas to be included then it is easy to offer alternatives to them such as the consultation board.

The inside of a Talking and Thinking Floorbook™

Spoons

There are occasions when the starting point for the discussion happens at the snack area. In this case the adult, rather than a child, called the meeting.
A child was interested in the way that he could see his reflection in the back of the metal spoon. This generated a small group discussion where they all looked at their spoons and remarked on their appearance.
"Mine's got goo on it"
"Lick it off and then you have got lines on your face'

" I can't see me"
" I can see you…in my spoon…"
"Why am I in your spoon?"

The conversations were wide and varied but most seemed to focus on the spoons. It was apparent that children knew that there were a variety of spoons " for babies", " for grandpa's sore hands", " for having a cup of tea", "for eating Petit Filouuuus". The children went onto comment that nursery only had the see through ones (plastic teaspoons).

Children moving circles around to sort the spoons

The adult decided to call a meeting to discuss what spoons the children wanted to get for the snack area. As with any meeting there were decisions to be made, note takers with clipboard/paper and special pens (shiny blue with feathery bits reserved for meetings!). The adult scribed too, stopping occasionally to clarify information with the 'note takers'. The children self selected to attend, most of the children in the group were 4/ 5 yrs old.

Children's ideas were based around food and how many things you could get in a spoon.
"We need big spoons for the raisins, always have to use my little spoons a lot"
"I want a Spiderman spoon"
"I like pink spoons and I like pink icing"

To support children and to widen their awareness of spoons the staff arranged a display of a range of spoons. When working with children I have always found it more effective to focus on experiences that are part of their lives. Exploration of tangible things often leads to greater engagement and deeper thinking.
This led to the use of the Bags of Discovery. The spoon one contains about 20 spoons. In addition to the simple household spoons it has extendable ones, love spoons, spurtles, tasting spoons, decorated spoons, tea caddy spoons the list goes on.

The children self selected to gather on the floor in one of the rooms. The provision of wicker or wooden rings lead children to try to organise the spoons. Some children

'Putting sets all together'

focused on the properties "These spoons are mirrors". Conversation focused on the features such as "this one has wobbly bits"(undulating surface that reflected her face), "these are jaggy"(spaghetti spoons in metal and wood). Other children gave their opinion and preference "My Gran likes these". When all the spoons were laid out and sorted into rings. We sat and looked. One of the children commented that the shiny spoons should all be together. The second child said that "that can't be, I have Grans spoon here. It is not going with you" The conversation ranged around trying to find a solution. In the end a third child put the two rings on top of each other and put all the metal ones in there (including Gran's spoon) "there now they can all be together". A physical approach to Venn Diagrams.

The children were motivated by sorting and classifying the spoons so the next session they found a circle of spoons and only four circles in the centre. One child approached the challenge from the angle of materials, others put a number in each, others explored the spoons and didn't put them in any circle.

Holly and Lauren decided to sort them into 'the same as' ones. Tana found a purple spoon in the kitchen, so brought it to the table, to sort.

Spoons to explore

A limited number of circles to encourage problem solving

The experience had started with a group discussion, moved into a meeting and then naturally flowed into the opportunities in the centre.

Children need to be physically involved in their thinking. A group of four girls took out the circular place mats that were often used for sorting activities. They sat together and were obviously looking at the circles. Their conversation went as follows;

"We don't have enough."
"What ? Blue ones ?"
"No we need more yellow ones."
"No more of all of them."
"How can we do it then ?"
"We will have to make them smaller."
"What smaller ?"
"Those ones were tiny, too small to have a cup of tea."
"No, the way we do it."

At this point they came to me to get the bag of spoons. The more dominant child in the group had been talking about 'needing more spaces' then started to lead the play. Asking questions such as 'Can we put little shiny and the little wood together ?' She appeared to have been thinking through the idea that if there were only nine circles, some of the sets would have to be combined to give a smaller number of sets. The quieter children in the group followed her lead and started to combine groups of spoons onto the mats. The categories they used became more abstract as the session went on. The creativity involved in the sorting process was generated through the group discussion, as children began to become more confident the quieter members of the group offered their ideas. The categories they suggested included;

"You can get them in the Co-op"
"My granny's got them"
"My baby sister likes playing with them"
"My mum gave me one to use in the garden"
"These are fairy spoons"
"I could hide these in my dolls house"
"These are paddles for my Action man"
All these ideas are accepted as evidence of thinking.

- **Writing as part of a group can support children to make marks and communicate with greater confidence.**
- **Children communicate in a variety of ways that can be celebrated through collaborative experiences.**
- **Some children prefer individual experiences & ways of communicating.**

The idea that we all write together, at the same time, to share the writing process came from a project called 'Write to learn' in Wiltshire, that I was part of at the start of my career. We can demonstrate so much to children by joining them in the processes of exploring and recording. It is a strategy that works with all people from 3 to 93. Group cohesion can give people real confidence.

The group writing can model that to be a writer we need to;
Be able to make marks,
Write in a direction,
Consider that different styles of writing use the page differently, and of course pencil grip and secretarial skills, but also that when we think ...

Children recording ideas

We can change our minds.
We can learn from each other.
We can think and not have to speak.
We can communicate in many different ways.
We can be an individual with our own ideas.
We can write our ideas down and they will be valued by the group.
We can think and feel good about our own ideas.
We can understand our own writing and drawings.
We can talk about what we think and that it will actually affect something.
We can plan and draw so that we can change what we do in our play.

Talking about ideas within the community of a group

The group writing approach was used by many adults as the first stage in planning many years ago. It was creative then and it is now, children will give their ideas freely. Some of the challenges we face in group writing are linked to the management of children. This initial writing may take place in a group session, the group may be self selected or selected for the interest shown.

Through giving each child a different coloured pen we can monitor the contributions from a particular child. If Joanne is using pink and has made a tiny squiggle, I would support her by talking on a one to one basis during the main play session. Her thinking could

then be put on an individual thinking bubble. This can then be stuck into the book to share her thinking with the other children. Likewise when children over dominate the conversation we need to help them be aware of the effect of their exuberance. The use of individual talking and thinking books or perhaps a personal pocket can allow the children to extend the amount they write without dominating the group session.

Group writing can take place in the main play session alongside the play. An example of this can be seen in the case study around bridges. By lining the walls around a area such as construction we are able to use them for consultation and thinking. In a good construction area there will be photographs of building types,

old building plans, tools of construction, paintbrushes to complete the décor, tape measures in a variety of styles and a place to draw. It can be the walls. I do not believe that having drawn on paper all children are going to go away and be graffiti artists. When children are playing the writing is purposeful. If there are children who wish to destroy or deface they will do that anyway. Use gridded paper, paper with a starting bubble in the middle, paper that has the start of a building, paper with measurements simply marked on. These are the pebbles in the

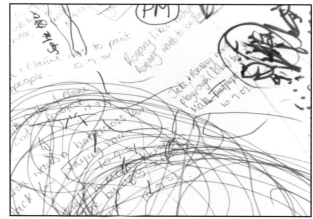

Consultation in den building area

water, they will stimulate interest and are wide enough that they allow children to take the play where they wish. At the end of the process I take down papers and fold them to fit in a large pocket at the back of the book to show the process of development.

The Body Book

Many children are motivated by their own bodies. They are a constant source of fascination and interest as they change. In the following pages I have used examples from a number of Talking and Thinking Floorbooks™ which started for a variety of reasons.

A child fell over and was distraught about "The blood leaking out" - The Centre decided to explore the way blood moves around the body. Children used tubing, bandages, red jelly and cotton wool as part of the play and discovery.

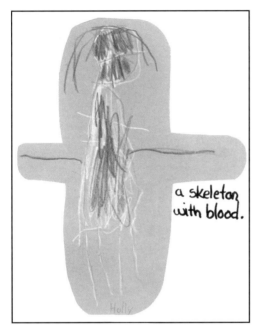

a skeleton with blood.

When asked the question - "What's inside our bodies ?", this is what some of the children replied.
Eva: *"You have blood in your body"*
David: *"I have a skeleton, it makes us move, and a heart it goes boom and blood is all round my body."*
Ben: *"I've got bones because I'm a boy, girls don't have bones they only have backs."*
Louise: *"Muscles, muscles are your strength. We use our muscles at the mini kickers"*
Naddia: *"You have babies in your body"*
Eva: *"I know what's in your head, a brain so you can think"*
Jack: *"My brain's in my tummy."*

In another Centre there was an interest in earrings and body piercing - in a short session that lead to the creation of a book, the children were asked "What are ears for ?" The Talking and Thinking Floorbook™ lead to a change of direction in their planning to 'explore different types of ears'. The children were asked "Why do we have ears"

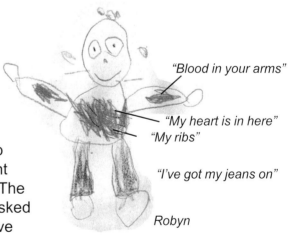

"Blood in your arms"

"My heart is in here"
"My ribs"

"I've got my jeans on"

Robyn

Here are some of the replies.
Alan: *"Cos they go on the side of yer head."*
Fiona: *"Cos we don't."*
Matthew: *Because we can't hear without ears."*
Gemma: *"Because that's why I'm here."*
Kirstie: *"I've got ears."*
Keiran: *"To talk frew a telephone."*
Lana: *"To hear with."*
Connor: *"Cos, ooh, I don't know, for your earrings"*

Many children are fascinated by the way that the blood moves around the body. When children talk about their ideas through a group session, they often reveal frameworks of understanding that enable them to make sense of the world around them. The challenge for the adult is that in order to be child centred in their planning they have to be responsive and think on their feet. Through recording thinking through group writing we can revisit their ideas over time to monitor if their ideas have been followed through or acknowledged.

Freedom to follow their own investigations

Exploring flow

The children in these photographs were playing in nurseries that were part of a long-term course that was exploring the Talking and Thinking Floorbooks™ as a mode of formative assessment. The children were interested in the veins, capillaries and arteries and the concept that they were tubes running all over your body. In response to this the adults provided tubes in the water tray. This experience has been replicated elsewhere and the same focus was evident, in the latter case the adults coloured the water red. Children asked for some tubes by name such as capillaries and veins. The arteries were called 'big gushers', probably in response to a medical drama on the television. The staff put a variety of tubes into the water tray from 5mm diameter to 20mm.

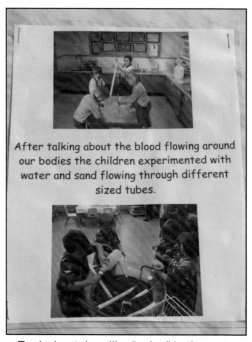
After talking about the blood flowing around our bodies the children experimented with water and sand flowing through different sized tubes.

Exploring tubes like "veins" in the water area

The children used the stimulus of the red water to great effect, as they tried to 'stop the blood' or to 'mop the blood from the floor'. The experience of playing in the water tray with tubes had a great emotional connection to the children. Many of the children stayed in the area for many weeks. The ideas had been created by the group thinking at the start of the interest, and had been supported by adult provision of time, resources and space. As a facilitator in the first group writing session the adult could support the sharing of ideas so that children could feed their ideas directly into the planning.

- **Talking and Thinking Floorbooks™ can allow each child to share their thinking in a way that is appropriate to their learning style and cultural experience.**
- **Strategies such as Talking Tubs™, Talking and Thinking Trees™ are designed to appeal to a range of learners so that everyone reaches their potential.**
- **All people have a motivational button. Practitioners need to find it in themselves and the children they work with.**

Supporting individuals

Children work to their own agenda, many calmly moving across boundaries and making connections that are not detailed on any planning sheet. This is the way that learning happens, it is an integrated process with no curricular boundaries. In the early years we educate children to explore and investigate, the actual facts they are taught are often secondary to the skills and attitudes they develop in a positive learning environment. Since the majority of children seem to flow along and core experiences support their play the planning can become focused on their interests and behaviours. It is often these experiences that are recorded as an interest in the Talking and Thinking Floorbooks™.

'Being given time to explain'

However there are some children who are individuals and learn in their own way and are often singular in their focus. The Talking and Thinking Floorbooks™ should include their ideas and how they have followed through their ideas in play. We need an environment that allows young children to follow through their interests and ideas whilst we use the scaffold of a curriculum to monitor breadth and balance. The opportunities that are on offer in some centres can focus on the group in the middle of a continuum and not offer support for those children at the start of the process and those that require challenge to maintain their involvement.

In environments where there is often a high degree of adult direction there would have to be phenomenal assessment and recording to make sure that the level and subjects offered meet the exact needs of all the individuals in the centre. Given that this would involve copious amounts of record keeping it could detract from the core role of the adult, which to me, is to interact with children in order to facilitate learning through exposition or enquiry. In a consultative environment the open ended nature of the experiences ensures that there is differentiation through the outcome of the play, so there does still need to be an awareness of the level and interest of the group but since the adult is not over directing, the children's ownership automatically gives a closer match to their needs.

There are number of ways that the individual can be supported through the Talking and Thinking Floorbooks™;

❖ Involvement through individual pockets or envelopes set within the floorbook. For some children contributing in a group situation is inappropriate. Some children are egocentric in the way they work and prefer to create their own little books in the writing area. These can then be taken by the child and put into their own personal envelope. Some of the books are scribed and others are left as the child's mark making. By putting a photograph on the front we can support children to be independent in finding their own envelope in the book.

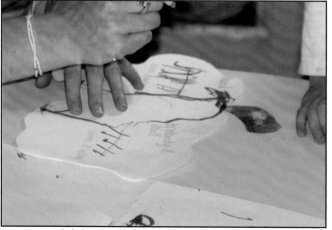

Individual interests can stimulate the group

❖ Kinaesthetic children learn through movement both small and large scale. To respond to this we can ask children;

  ○ To work on the Talking and Thinking Tree as they move around the area during the play session.
  ○ To share thinking when they are outside on consultation boards.
  ○ To share ideas on large outdoor Talking and Thinking Trees so they can run and from the tree.
  ○ To share their ideas as they walk or crawl around the Talkaround Mat™
  ○ To engage with 3D talking tubs so they can handle objects and talk at the same time.

❖ The books are part of the community of learning and as such are available to children throughout the session. Children can record their ideas in the writing area and put the sheets into the book at any point in the learning process.

❖ The learning styles that we have already explored influence our preferences for the way that we record notes. The standard bullet pointed list, lines of narrative, subheadings, and forms with grids are all functional and precise. They do appeal to people who enjoy order, sequence and precision. These traits can be seen with children, as children choose squared paper and proceed to fill each square with a mark. But what about the other children who respond to colour, visual patterns and connections, and respond well to pictures? Well, they may enjoy using paper that is abstract shapes

Adult recording as partners in learning

such as thinking bubbles, paper with stars on, or radial lines. Through the provision of a range of papers for the Talking and Thinking Floorbooks™ we can respond to individual preferences for note taking and recording in the learning environment.

❖ Tactile learners are often linked within kinaesthetic approaches and although it is connected I do consider it to be important enough to consider it on its own. When we are working with people under three we consult them through observing and then offering experiences, the whole environment is sensorial. As children mature, there seems to be a move to take them into spaces that are full of plastic coloured materials that offer less for the tactile learner. Through the use of sensorial resources for the Talking Tubs, offering sensorial materials in all areas of the play and allowing children to handle the book and create a textural cover we can respond effectively to their needs.

❖ Individual interests can stimulate the whole group to follow a lead. The example shown was one little girl who was actually very reserved, who came in to the centre wanting to create a duck pond. The process of consultation put her idea in the centre of the Talkaround and the effect on her perception of herself was marked. She would re-visit the book and look at all the photographs long after the nursery group had moved on to other interests.

❖ Many people ask me what do you do if key children dominate the talk. As with all interactions it is our role to bring forward the less dominant and give them additional status by supporting their ideas. This may be through statements of observations such as' when I was in the construction area today I noticed how carefully Jason built a tower, his idea to make each brick fit exactly was very clever' or through sharing photographs, or offering the child a chance to speak. Dominant children sometimes need other ways of sharing the huge amount they know, perhaps through individual books, or a consultation sheet on an easel.

❖ When I was working with a group with the talking and thinking tree it became apparent that although the interest of the group at the start of the process appeared to be food, when the discussion started the actual focus of the group was dinosaur food!

Children had leaves spread out over the table and had started to make marks when one of the boys said "my food is for my dinosaur, I can't draw all his teeth so I am going to draw a smile". That was it. As in all transformational play the drawings changed their meaning.

"the food was stolen by dinosaurs"
"mine is a pink dinosaur who lives in flowers and he likes riding a bike"
"I know where there is a skeleton of a dinosaur…in the plant by the door"

"There is a big one with bits on his back and one that was tiny like a baby"

They had a huge amount of knowledge. It is at this point that the practitioner has to make a choice, should they continue with their identified interest or follow the children's lead. Dinosaurs is the one subject that young children find hugely interesting even though it is impossible to give a first hand opportunity! The leaves included a wide range of mark making and many children were very involved in the process of hanging leaves on the tree.

'Helping to reach the top of the tree'

Collecting connected objects for the tree

As the session evolved children moved around the nursery gathering three-dimensional objects to add to the tree. Dinosaurs were gathered, bones, pictures, food for them to eat the collection grew and as each piece was included in the pile the children could connect it.

The challenge for some child-initiated ideas is that they can become repetitive. The adults were aware that dinosaurs could lead to very aggressive play that was often repetitive in its outcome. To challenge these children and encourage

children to engage in wider thinking the adults decided to explore the habitats of dinosaurs. With a wider knowledge the adults gained they were able to offer dinosaurs in herds, some in forests in the materials tray with lumps of wood, some in sand and water with grass and mud for the swamp dwellers. Dinosaurs were put in situations, which showed scale. Small dinosaurs were taken outside and put in small world zones at the base of trees, or near rocks.

Children adding 3D objects to the tree

A windy day

Like all people, children all have different 'motivational buttons'. The skill of a facilitator is to ensure that everyone feels the desire to contribute, are able to contribute and engage in a way that is appropriate and meaningful to him or her. This case study took place in an outside area where children were able to choose and select items in a free way, to reflect the self help methodology inside the centre. It was a windy day and the children were already motivated to go outside.

'A Windy Day'

Movement based learning

I was working with a group of children when a gust of wind came and lifted my hair. We talked about the way it felt when the wind 'played' with your hair. Shaking our heads to move our medium/ long hair. I turned around to see a boy standing moving his head. "I can't feel it". We realised that he had a very short haircut and was therefore not able to empathise with our description. One of the children offered to make him a wig, 'just like her grandma'. The group moved to an area outside which provided wool, ribbon and masking tape. They all made wigs and wore them for the rest of the session. This was followed up with the introduction of wear a wig week. The centre offered each child a glitter wig to keep. The whole of the week some boys wore their glitter wig. The same boy that had played with us at the start said, "it was long like.. shaky on your head…it went into my mouth and I would have it cut off'.

In order to respond to individuals we need to offer a range of pathways that enable them to explore the same concept in a variety of ways. In centres were checklists are followed and ticked off as children 'do' an activity, the pathway can become very direct and structured. Adults need to monitor the overall experiences, but I would question the need for all children to do all the activities on offer.

On the windy day some children drew pictures on clipboards when they were outside. The movement of the wind was transferred into the movement of the pencil on the paper. Raindrops were presented by the way they felt when they landed on their heads, as a dot. These responsive pictures were folded up and put into pockets 'to help them remember' and some went into the Talking and Thinking Book®.

One of the children took the paper off the clipboard and let it go. This re-focused many children to running around 'with the wind' trying to catch the white paper. When the children were talking about the experience they retold it in a kinaesthetic way, unable to divide speech and movement. Getting up from the Talkaround Mat™ he moved about whilst he spoke "The wind went wooooh wooooh and then big drops came. We ran and ran and ran until my legs hurt, then I had to hop."

To take this experience forward the staff put together a box of lightweight holographic wrapping paper that was plastic so that it could withstand being in mud and floating on top of puddles. The papers were about half a metre square to allow children to waft them and feel the breeze as well to feel the movement.

A little boy had said in the Floorbooks that he liked dancing in the wind. When asked where he thought it would be good to dance he said "by the fence". Another little girl asked if they could use the ribbons that had been used in the weaving.

When they went outside they tied the ribbons into the fence. The adults had considered possible lines of development and had included lightweight ribbons, and also heavier strips of fabric like felt and bubble wrap. By doing this they were able to encourage exploration of the strength of the wind. When the wind blew they waited for it to lift the ribbons and then they danced, the game evolved to running through without being touched. One boy asked why the chain never moved (a length of metal chain was still on the fence from a previous game). The children displayed varying degrees of interest. They said "because its too big", "don't know…lets dance again", " 'cos it doesn't want to". The first boy continued to stand by and watch, as the wind moved the materials up and down. When I went over I talked to him about the fact that there was a man called Beaufort who noticed the same thing, that some things moved and others didn't. He decided to give the wind a number, so we know how strong it is. After a brief conversation we went our

'Dancing in the wind'

separate ways, as I was walking away I heard him say "See that Beaufort, he lives round the corner from me!' As a result of talking about the Victorian scientist who created the Beaufort scale, the children started to not only to draw the weather, but to give it a number according to 'how big' they thought it was. The numbers varied from 'nothing' to "seventy hundred" all of which were valued and written into a book that held the 'talking we do when we talk about clouds and that'. Children could choose to write on gridded paper, abstract shapes, lines, dots, and hearts in order to respond to their preferences. There were numbers, forms and suggestions of graphs interwoven into the book that some children sought out. This gave far more individuality to the experience than an adult designed sheet. The plans showed extended blocks of time both inside and outside engages in weather recording.

The windy spell continued over a few days enabling children to explore it a variety of ways. Children attached windmills to the handlebars of their bikes to measure 'how fast the wind was going by'; others danced with streamers, some struggled to lash down a den. The variety of experience allowed children to follow their interest, the planning recorded some individual responses but not all, as this would become unsustainable. The skill lies in the constant monitoring of whether the resources on offer will enable individuals to achieve what they want, rather than only complete the adult activity.

- **Visualisation can boost the brains' ability to remember information.**
- **Affirmation provided by the feedback loop of putting objects on a tree, encourages children to share more.**
- **The Talking & Thinking Tree focuses children in a visual, kinaesthetic and sensorial way. The talk alongside, stimulates the auditory sense.**
- **Children's ideas can be sorted along physical 'lines of thought' to make planning more coherent.**

Through working with young children, and those that respond to movement based learning, it became apparent that there was a need to create a way for children to share their ideas whilst being on the move. The Talking and Thinking tree can be an artificial tree or a real one. Its purpose is to focus the children on a point so that gathering their ideas becomes a physical, active process rather than a sedentary one.

Talking & Thinking Tree

Tree decorating is an important part of our culture. We have kept the tradition of Christmas trees since Victorian times, but before that when people were in tune with seasonal variations they dressed and decorated real trees.

It was this desire to hang objects on a tree that first inspired me to look at the potential of a tree that could be used as a tree of knowledge.

How to introduce the concept.

Children are very responsive and in many centres and schools there is an automatic understanding of the symbol of a tree and how we should use it. In other situations I have had to create an appropriate atmosphere and clear expectations when working with children. The expectations are not laid down in stone but they do set parameters and let children know what behaviours are valued. The way I do this is through storytelling.

The appearance & care of materials gives a positive message.

Storytelling is a very large part of the work we do. It enables children to enter a place where they can explore and experiment with their ideas in a situation that is called suspended disbelief. Through engaging in a story it shields them from a reality that can be affected by adult opinion. There are children in our education systems that have already gathered a message that they are 'not able' rather than 'enabled' to do something. The emotional aspects of the approach are very important. To be able to try an idea that you have had gives a huge impetus to the link between self worth and learning.

The story that I tell mentions the key attitudes that we are trying to encourage such as trying hard, working together, thinking about ideas and not worrying about being right all the time. The story journey is designed to orientate and support children by mentioning some aspects of the subject we are talking about. An example may be evidence of caterpillars, or small eggs under a leaf, an area full of half eaten fruit which all relate to butterflies. If children are motivated by the story they may well remember facts since they were engaged on an emotional level. The story takes them to a tree in a clearing that is presented as a tree of knowledge, but strangely it never has any leaves! The offer of a challenge usually works and children cannot resist creating a thinking leaf to create a 'Tree of Knowledge'.

Decorating the Talking and Thinking Tree™

How do you 'manage' the children?

The tree is placed on a table with no chairs around it so that they can move around the tree as they talk and think. The adult shapes the leaves at first; otherwise the cutting becomes the focus rather than the thinking and recording. The children go onto create their own leaves as they become more comfortable with the idea. A hole punch allows children to create their own holes and hang them on the tree.

Any new strategy stimulates interest from a group of children. At first the interest takes over the thinking. Gradually as the novelty wears off children integrate the strategies into the main play room.

The feeling of achievement must be powerful, since often reluctant writers will create leaf after leaf just to hang them on the tree. The feedback loop is immediate and encourages them to keep on recording their thinking. There is no specific task for young children to complete, it is a process that is voluntary and should not be forced.

Children require a range of stimuli to interest and stimulate them to engage in the process. There are a number of issues to consider;

- ❖ The position of the tree. On the floor, or on a low table

- ❖ Time the group and individuals have to access the tree. In a circle at key times, available all the time in the play room, short blocks at set times such as every month or every week.

- ❖ Adult interaction. Organised and focused by the adult, initiated by the children, or based on observation.

Those children who are stimulated by the visual aspect of their surroundings do focus on the appearance of the tree. The artificial trees are copper and silver coloured.

Kinaesthetic children move and leap around it talking and singing as they go. Auditory learners share stories and talk about all manner of things that go on the tree. The tactile experiences are supplied through the texture of the tree and the process of mark making and manipulation of the paper.

Extensions and variations;

❖ The tree can be used to explore small 3D objects. These may be part of the Talking Tub™ related to the subject. E.g. winter may have small snowmen, scarves, and chains of snowflakes to hang on the tree.

❖ Complete the Talking and Thinking tree in a special place such as the dark den, write by torchlight, hang glow in the dark snowflakes on the winter tree and look at the ideas shine in the dark.

Talking and thinking about mathematics

The creation of the tree is free flowing and children are not highly structured when they take part. The very youngest children are exploring the idea that they can write and think, which should be a lot of fun.
Older children begin to reason and consider, bringing their knowledge and understanding of the world to share with adults and peers. Children should be encouraged to see themselves as confident writers with something to say. It is this aspect of early writing that we should celebrate rather than the secretarial skills.

Lines of thought

The ideas that children put on the tree are very wide. The first step will be to gather ideas that can then be sorted either by children along strings (lines of thought) or by the adult at planning meetings.
The subject that provides most 'leaves' is one that obviously offers a greater bank of existing knowledge and is therefore the point I start from. With a bank of knowledge, children feel more secure and able to contribute to any process of consultation.

Children have a great ability to develop an understanding of the world around them; they will share it in a way that makes sense to them which is often not in the language or style that adults use. The Talking and Thinking tree is a strategy that allows kinaesthetic children to engage in learning at any stage of education.

Strategies for recording on the leaves

The benefits are detailed to the side of the photograph.

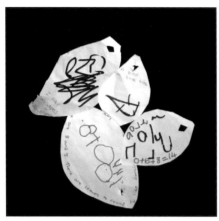

Child's writing with adult scribing

- Partnership between child and adult.
- Individual marks.
- Accessible to all adults, after the play experience.
- Older child can scribe.
- Dated for reference.

- Very individualistic.
- Greater independency.
- Limited understanding of adults 'reading' marks after the play experience.

Children's writing

Adult recording children's talk

- Can give affirmation regarding 'the amount' written on the leaf.
- Rapid and accurate.
- Older child can scribe.
- Dialect and structure recorded.
- Dated for reference.
- Talking & thinking occurs without concern for secretarial skills.

- Observation of group.
- Observation of individual.
- Rapid and accurate.
- Analysis of observation can link to all leaves above.
- Dated for reference.

Adult recording observations of play

Outdoor trees

The consultation process should take place in all aspects of the centre, the outside is just another space without walls and a ceiling. It should be given the same thought and planning as inside so that both areas are of equal importance. Consultation will give a greater meaning to the opportunities in the outside area so that they link and flow to the inside and back outside.

We have created a range of strategies that can be used in any outdoor area.

❖ Create an enclosure of trees that will give an atmosphere of peace and calm, that supports the thinking process.

❖ Identify one living tree in a quieter area or settling zone that has many soft branches at a child's height so that children can hang their ideas on it.

❖ If the trees have a wide girth and the branches start high up, use a removable string or ribbon around the tree. Make the leaves with double paper so that they can 'hang' over the ribbon. Another alternative would be to tie laminated leaves to the ribbon around the tree so that the end leaf can be written on by children standing on the ground.

❖ Create spirals and forms in willow that can be hung down from the tree branch for children to hang leaves with loops on.

❖ Create a pretend tree from a painted branch. Monitor the ends of the branches in case they become too brittle.

❖ Create outdoor leaves from encapsulated skeleton leaves, or real leaves. Use a dry board marker to write on them.

❖ Outdoor leaves can be created with any old wrapping paper, perhaps linked to the seasonal colours.

Creating outdoor Talking and Thinking trees gives the adults an opportunity to share photographs, ideas, objects just as inside.

Laminated real leaves

Laminated leaves

Where do the leaves go ?

As with most aspects of a child's play the process is transient. We encourage children to create their own tree in the Talking and Thinking Book so that they can retain their ideas. Leaves are stuck in any way the children wish. Some children want their leaves all in one place; others strive to put them at the top of the tree!
Children will record a great deal on the leaves the approach is successful. If their ideas are important to them some of the children will want to take them home, others enjoy the process but do not feel the need to keep the product.

The emphasis on this approach is that the process of consultation feeds into the content of the planning sheets. If children are giving ideas that link to a group interest this may well affect the subject of the Talking and Thinking Book. If the umbrella interest is all Minibeasts the consultation may show a smaller, in depth focus on Slugs.

The leaves on the tree may contain;
*   ❖ Ideas for activity such as 'I want to make a bed for mine',
*   ❖ Observations such as 'look... its all slimy and yuk',
*   ❖ Thoughts such as 'I think a mummy has lots of babies'
*   ❖ Questions such as ' How do they stick on?'
*   ❖ Drawings
*   ❖ Mark making that actually demonstrates movement or sound
*   ❖ Free mark making to explore the process rather than a greater link to thinking about a subject.

Tree drawn by the children inside the floorbook. Children cover the tree with their leaves

The leaves are the same as the bubble shaped paper I use in the general playroom in that they have a great deal of value both to adults as forms of formative assessment, but also to the children. There is an implicit message which we send to them, through the way that we handle and present their work and treat their ideas and that is, when we value children, we value their work. It is therefore important that we keep some of their leaves.

There are a number of possible solutions;

*   ❖ Individual pockets in the large Talking and Thinking Floorbook™ to keep little books and individual thinking leaves.
*   ❖ Create a tree in the book with the children that can then be covered by the leaves. Many leaves are covered on both sides, so an adult may need to help with 'hinging'.
*   ❖ Children have individual Talking and Thinking Floorooks that are used to keep the leaves and any individual ideas. This tends to be used more in the 5-11 age group so that it can be used in contextualised play areas.
*   ❖ Children can have a page each in a larger book so that individual thinking is easier to track. This does make it harder to follow how group thinking develops through listening to each other.

Talking and Thinking Floorbooks™

Case study for Talking & Thinking Trees

Numeracy

This case study is focused on how we can encourage children to share their thinking with us about any aspect of the curriculum.

When working with mathematics I often find that children feel restricted by the resources and schemes that are being introduced at earlier and earlier points in the

Winter tree with numbers

education system. Several years ago I worked with schools and centres in Perth and Kinross council to explore children's understanding of mathematics and to develop strategies that were not only consultative but also motivational.

The Talking and Thinking Tree proved to be one of the strategies that supported children to share what they understood about mathematics. This case study is set in the winter term in a playgroup that had to clear away the furniture twice a week.

We have already discussed how important it is to the consultation process that children's ideas are valued. When I asked children 'What numbers are in your head?' they all started to chant "1,2,3,4,5, until their voices got quieter and stopped" "they are super numbers, but I am sure that there may be some more." Pause. One boy put up his hand " I know a number…a million!" his friend sitting next to him said, " I know bigger than him. A million and one" The children were 3 to 4 years old. They had a huge amount of knowledge about mathematics and number, but in the context of a worksheet or formalised questioning, " What number is this?" the knowledge did not transfer. Children told me numbers in their heads like 'forty ninety eighty and three', ideas they had for building 'a shop with hundreds of shoes', they used materials and skills in play that far exceeded those expected by curricular documents. By consulting children we can share their knowledge about number and mathematics through problems that arise through play for example How long should we play on the computer? or How many raisins shall we have at snack?

The Talking and Thinking Tree was presented to the group through a storytelling session. The story was made up to allow children to give ideas and solutions within the tale for example Grandpa teddy bear forgot the phone number of Jo the Ted, which direction to turn? How many steps will he take? The children are already engaged and gathering ideas and confidence through the protective atmosphere of a story. There are always problems left unsolved in the story, such as what roofing materials to use, or how to make a waterproof pair of Wellington boots.

Icicles, snowflakes and numbers on the tree

At a point in the story the travellers come upon a tree. The storyline is designed to support feelings of affirmation, visualisation and positive thinking. The text follows this line. 'The tree was standing alone in a clearing. As the travellers moved closer they saw to their amazement that it was a tree of knowledge. But there were no leaves, not one. They looked all around to try to find the knowledge. As they looked drawings and pictures started to appear on all the leaves around them. Reaching down they had the most amazing feeling as the ideas and thoughts came streaming into their heads.'

As children open their eyes, or start moving I suggest that if they have ideas in their heads that they should put it on our tree of knowledge for everyone to share. They may have things they want to do, or things that they want to find out, or maybe just share what they know already. The strategy is so flexible that it moves across from formative assessment to planning very naturally. There were ideas for making the ice queens den on one tree, on another it may be counting and sorting icicles, with some ideas about where they are from. The sorting and classifying of ideas and next steps for action, takes place when the leaves are stuck into the Talking and Thinking Floorbooks™.

With younger children the story is short and after making marks on their 'leaves' they move onto exploring the baskets and box that goes with the tree. Some have already reached the point where marks have an associated meaning, for others it is the mark itself and the social community of learning that is the key aspect. Very young children can be consulted and often respond very well to positive role models. Given the time of year the box contained pretend icicles, snowflakes, silver chains of different lengths, a variety of fir cones sprayed and natural,

and metal snowflakes. The overall objective was mathematics with a numeric focus. The story, leaves and talk all influence the way the children move onto decorate the tree. Icicles were arranged in groups with numbers beside. Some were sorted onto a variety of branches 'these are the nice ones', 'these are pointed' and 'these are furry'. Some children contributed scientific knowledge 'I like the ice when it is slippy and we have a sledge', 'the ice is from the freezer' and 'Can we make some lollies?'

To offer challenge within the environment additional materials can be offered through a second bag such as a suitcase to match the tree. If I want to consult children about mathematics then there are props ready to use, such as the numeric waistcoat, or a thinking cap (decorated like a brain!). Both were home made and seem to create an approach that in drama would be called 'working within a mantle of the expert'. If children use imaginative play to move from being someone who doesn't know to someone who does then it will undoubtedly affect their emotional intelligence and feeling of engagement. The Talking and Thinking tree became a focus for the session.

- Consultation boards enable children to share ideas at any point in the session.
- The boards can be used in a variety of ways - pictorial, blank, inside and outside to respond to learning styles.
- Consultation boards can be used for any area of the curriculum.

Children can gather their ideas and share their thinking at any point in the play session through the use of consultation boards. The way that the board is presented is flexible. The underlying aspect is that children understand that their ideas are valued in which ever way they wish to share them. Drawing, diagrams, a variety of genre of writing, and photographs all have a place.

Thinking about any aspect of the curriculum should be displayed

Some options are;

❖ Sheets of paper mounted onto easels so that children can put down their thinking about any aspect of the curriculum. The example to the right is numeracy. These sheets can then be taken down and included in the Talking and Thinking Floorbook™ as evidence of exploration and thinking.

❖ White card can be used so that the board can go in and out on fair weather days.

❖ Laminate blank card, or card with symbols on to stimulate children to write. All weather option to go outside.

❖ White boards allow children to modify ideas rapidly but adults need to record the work through photographs if they wish to keep a record.

❖ Portable whiteboards enable children to carry their ideas from inside to out and visa versa. Can be photocopied to gather evidence.

❖ 'Post it notes" can be used although, if the board becomes popular, they do have a tendency to drop off.

Consultation board with child drawings

Children can be encouraged to record their thinking in any way they wish although some children who need some encouragement may enjoy the stimulation of a variety of blank markings on the board such as bubbles, central mind map shapes, grids, boxes, swirls and circles. It is worth watching how children use the different forms. A group that had a pretend stable outside had horses' heads to ride. At the end of the 'stable block' the adults had put up A3 laminates of forms and shapes for outdoor mark making.

The ability to reflect on your own ideas and talk yourself through challenges or even general exploration has a direct effect on the way your brain processes ideas and faces challenges. Consultation boards can be used to record ideas by one child or by a few. The example on the outside boards was one little girl who wanted to make a den. The photograph in the centre of the board was of a woven tipi that another child had lashed

together. "I want to make a house, but not like that. I want a flat space like this (draws round shape on board) " then I will put a bedroom here and that's the place the dog is..I know that would be good because I am thinking dogs like a place like that" (draws smaller circle at the top.) " I will eat in it and then I want to put a red roof like this " (draws thick horizontal red line).

When you consider that all of us have an inner voice it is hardly surprising that children find it far easier to talk themselves into and out of a situation. Children are affected by their emotions and can ebb and flow very rapidly. Where a child has 'a voice' that is supportive and analytical it can create a very positive way of approaching learning. When the inner voice is full of doubt it can affect the child's ability to reach their potential.

Call and Smith (2003) suggest that children use something called pole bridging, both verbal and diagrammatic in order to make sense of what people are saying to them. This link from what the child already knows and the new information is critical in many educational models. What appears to be harder to define is how to do it, within the early years setting. It is this aspect that I do through the Talking and Thinking Floorbooks™. The books show progression in thinking and allow children to consult each other, the boards give all children a chance to contribute to the book at any point in the session.

The other way to use a consultation board is in the process of discussion with children. An adult can create a consultation board by using images that children can look at. An example would be the room layout of the nursery. Many adults create the layout of the nursery in a way that makes sense to them. When children look at photographs of the areas and we ask them where they want an object to go, such as the sand tray, they will suggest it 'should be next to the water' so that they mix the two up. Yet many centres have rules that the two are not even allowed in the same room, never mind meet and actually mix!! Through consultation we can make informed choices and decisions. We do need areas and zones, but the process of consultation with children allows children to share their views and make selected choices that matter to them.

Once the ethos of consultation comes into the centre it is important that it is an underpinning attitude so that staff are consulted in the process. The same techniques can be used for any age. Group writing, ideas on a consultation board allow all people to feel included and valued as part of the group.

- Children can be consulted through the routines such as making recipes.
- Children should be encouraged to make decisions about how and when they will complete their own plans.
- The consultation affects the content of the planning sheets through the integration of children's ideas.

Autonomy in the snack area encourages a great deal of independent skills. Through the process of consultation we can talk to children about rules and guidelines. In the Capers in the Kitchen file I wrote about the way that children can be given the

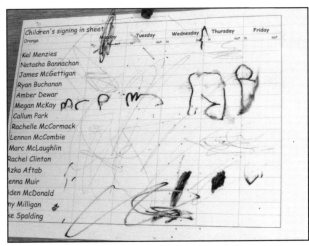

'Self registration' backed up by adult record

opportunity to create their own recipes. Some of the recipes are for us, and some for our feathered friends! Bird cake is a guaranteed success if we give children a range of types of seeds and nuts. The consultation involves thinking about how many spoonfuls each person feels that the bird might like. The responses are usually linked to colour such as' I am putting lots of them because they are like little bits and yellow', ' I want a handful of the brown ones, because they are big'. This process is almost inevitable and is pre-prepared by the adult through the P.L.O.D.S. (Possible Lines Of Development). The bird food needs to be at hand, and the children need to know what they have to choose from through the Talking Tub™. There is little point in asking a child what they would like in their bird cake and then not being able to provide it. The process of consultation provides greater ownership in the learning, it is exciting to have 35 different bird cakes that all look and work in different ways.

In this nursery the children have a self help café area, the adult allows the children to put up the number of items they can take for their snack as part of the mathematics opportunities. On this particular occasion it was a birthday party.

Charlie desperately wanted more than one of the cupcakes that they had made and the chocolate marshmallows but there was a number 1 above each plate indicating he could only have one of each ! He then looked in the numbers box and put up two number 2's - studied this for a minute and decided that he had another option, so took out the word 'Lots' which is used for snacks like raisins and stuck this above the plate with cupcakes. Had a look at it and decided he had done a good job !!!

This experience happened because they had empowered the children to think for themselves. They had been supported in simple decisions which had gradually become more challenging as the weeks went by. If the staff had not believed in consultation it would not have appeared as an opportunity in their planning and the children would not have thought to move labels and make decisions for themselves.

High Scope Planning.
The high scope approach has supported child led planning for many years. Children are encouraged to enter a cycle whereby they plan-do- and review their experiences. The example on the photographs was an individual planning sheet that child filled in I response to an interest in polar bears. The nursery were exploring winter time generally and this little girl wanted to look at polar bears and make one in the water tray. In response to this interest she found elements from a selection provided in drawers near by. In order to show the link between child's planning and actual activity, the nursery linked the planning and the photograph of play on the display board and then went on to put the notes into a folder heas evidence of consultation.
In a high quality high scope environment the ethos of consultation and the link that this has to the content of a planning sheet is evident. Children move through the environment with clear agendas that enable them to develop self motivation to explore and persevere with tasks. This high level of engagement is probably the same we see when children are consulted through the Talking and Thinking Floorbooks™. The opportunities follow an interest that they have initiated and therefore has a high sense of fulfilment.

High scope planning - plan, do, review

Talking and Thinking Floorbooks™

- **Children have clear opinions about situations that mean something to them.**
- **Adults can use strategies to enable children to give opinion.**

In centres that wish children to be active partners in a consultative environment there will be moments when a decision will have to be made. The process of decision making should be democratic and therefore should include a way of voting. The issue often lies in the management of the procedure so that children believe in the process.

Getting from a general view to a point that a decision can be made.

When children give their ideas we can create a map of their ideas, a grid, or a list. These ideas need to be categorised in order to make them manageable. By putting the ideas on separate pieces of paper we can move them around and put them into groups. For example if we record all of our ideas about plants some of the information

Consultation about the bird table

will be on their location, others their need, variety of appearances and so on. Once the ideas have been grouped we can then focus on a smaller element to make a decision on in this instance perhaps a new plant for the centre. This in turn raises a question as to whether a decision can be made if the brain has little knowledge of the options. At this point the adult may need to create a picture consultation board of the possibilities, in this case a selection of plants that are both affordable and accessible. Through discussions the adult can bring out the features of the plants or reinforce a child by reflecting on something they said at a previous session.

It should be noted that the subjects children want to make decisions about are not usually as mundane or predictable as the purchase of a plant.

In a small school in the north of Scotland a little boy was looking out of the window. A child who had just joined the nursery came up beside him and started to become very animated about the birds that were visiting the bird table. The conversation ranged from descriptions about the beaks to the number of birds that visited their bird table. "Why do the birds fly away?" Asked the youngest child. The 5 year old replied "Well, it's just because they are bored, nothing much to do". It was this conversation that encouraged the investigation into a bird table that was amusing for birds.

The adult wrote down their ideas in a talking and thinking book and since she had some awareness of a tape made in

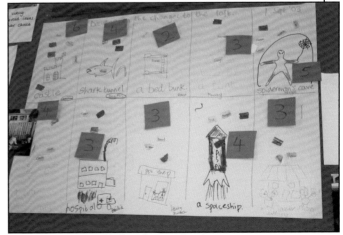
Voting for a role play area

Reggio Emilia in Italy about a similar interest, she was aware of the potential for learning.

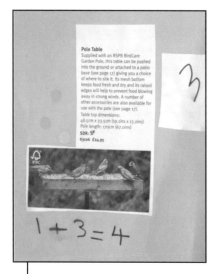

"Birds like to have music by other birds"
"They want a bath because when I am dirty my mum says I need a bath"
"Will they like bubbles?"
"They won't be able to swim because their legs are too thin."
"It's OK" (John left the area and went to the junk zone to gather some large elastic bands) "there, these are like my arm bands I have at the swimming pool"
"I like it when I get nice food"
"Surprise food would be great"

As the list went on several features came through such as a 'bath', 'bird song', 'a place to close your eyes safe from cats', and 'surprise food'.

Many of the items were created by the children in the construction area. When the children wanted to buy the actual bird table a selection of photographs from the catalogue were put together. The adult talked through the features and the costs of each.

Children can vote with a simple dot or a mark by an item of their choice. These dots were counted and the item with the most votes was ordered. The surprise food was designed to go down a tube from the nursery window to the table. The tube had a large enough diameter so that children could select from three or four buckets, and roll the food down onto the bird table. Even though the adult knew that this would scare away the birds, children were able to make some of the decisions in a democratic way.

Some of the decisions we make as adults can in fact be made by children. As effective practitioners we know that we can offer the early years curriculum through any or no context. The content can in fact naturally emerge through most contexts. In the photograph overleaf, entitled 'Voting for a role play area', a group of children were very interested in drama and performance and had spent some time investigating the possibilities for scenery and props. The adults had decided that it was time to change the role-play area and so gave the children the opportunity to change it in any way they wished. A consultation board was set up with eight of the children's ideas. Each child was

Gathering ideas outside on a laminated board

then given a label with their name on and put it beside the idea of their choice. At the end the dots were counted and the idea with the most names went forward to be the focus of the next aspect of consultation, which was to ask how they planned to build it. The process of voting and decision making covers a wide range of aspects of the curriculum and should be an integral part of any learning environment. Empowerment involves people in their learning which is an effective motivational button.

- ? Children have existing 'frameworks of understanding' that help them to make sense of the world.
- • Practitioners can challenge these 'frameworks' to deepen the knowledge and understanding skills and attitudes that are relevant and positive.

The first time I had a go at a talking and thinking book it was this one. So it is only fair that I include it in my book. I had been asked to gather ideas by a college lecturer some 20 years ago! It was decided that I should talk about electricity.

My first reaction had been one of disbelief, could the young children in the nursery really have any awareness of electricity? It was pointed out that if one were to follow this line of thought one might well end up limiting children through our own perceptions. A sound piece of advice.

So the scene was set. As the children entered the nursery we created an area called the Discovery Den that encouraged them to investigate. We provided a 5 volt, two prong battery and encouraged them to tell us what they could discover about the bulb. Our first challenge was to see if the bulb could light.

Creating lamps

The question "How can we light up the bulb ?" was put to the children

Luke: *"A magnet inside it helps make it work. Umm battery ... that silver metal and that gold metal and they stick together like this up on ceiling to see where you are going. Put sellotape on to make it stick. It getting hot because I touch it two times. I see wire inside battery electricity to get it to work. Electricity gets about because you wiggle the wire about. It crawls about, in wires."*

Richard: *"Don't know"*

Exploring bulbs, batteries & wires

The first statement took us by surprise. We had observed Luke as a little boy who enjoyed the Brio railway but had not really delved much further into what he knew. The book opened up all sorts of knowledge that we knew little about. The vocabulary, the ideas and concepts were all being explored as he played in the centre, and because we did not consult children we were oblivious to it!! It immediately changed our perceptions, the train set itself became more challenging because we put cargo loads into a tray so that the children could test the strength of the magnets by adding loads to the trailers.

The environmental displays became more scientific and we no longer limited ourselves to key words, the words that children used in the book became the precedent for discussion. The whole nursery became excited about what we could find out about the batteries and bulbs. Children started drawing at home and parents became engaged in the process, remarking on how the children seemed animated. Children made lamps from Rio Click and junk,

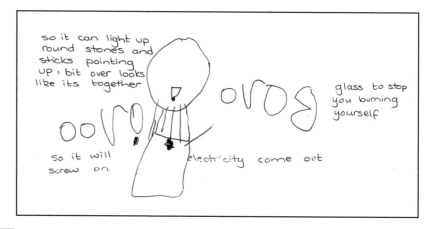

so it can light up round stones and sticks pointing UP, bit over looks like its together

glass to stop you burning yourself

so it will screw on

electricity come out

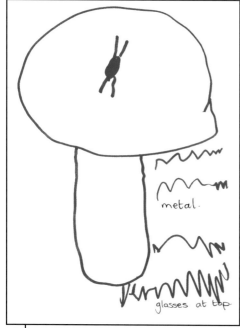

metal.

glasses at top.

children made circuits with crocodile clips mounted on boards and bulbs, diagrams were drawn and deep discussion took place.

After two years in the centre, we were aware that children needed more challenge. Children now talked of aluminium rather than 'metal', and contact points rather than the 'end bit'. The Discovery Den had allowed children to explore scientifically and then we had begun the process to listen to and look at the Frameworks of Understanding. Children had created ideas and principles that enabled them to find out about the world and understand how it was all connected.

We needed to remind ourselves that they were only 3-5 years old. That was the start of the process and I have been using and refining the process ever since!

In the autumn term many centres explore the concept of light and dark. Rather than finding a series of adult directed activities that vaguely connect to the theme, this centre set up a discovery den full of objects that use energy. The practitioner was close to the area and aware of their initial explorations. The large torch became the focus of interest. The children asked questions such as 'How does the light get in ?', 'Do all batteries fit the same thing ?' and 'How does it switch on ?'. In response to this observation the adults changed the discovery den to focus on torches and the different form of energy they use. The comments were used in the Talking & Thinking Floorbook™ as the starting point for a series of opportunities linked to the children's interest.

- Children can be effective designers of their own spaces.
- The process is more relevant if children can make informed choices and decisions.
- Children can affect planning through landscape use, resource provision or opportunity.

When we ask children what they would like outside, the experiences they hold in their brains is bound to influence their response. Some children repeat experiences to date, often 'bikes', others allow their imaginations to come to the fore and they request swimming pools, football pitches and dog homes !! The challenge that we face as adults is:

- How do we support children to make 'informed' choices without dictating to them ?
- How do we plan landscape and use outside, in a way that can actually come to fruition ?
- How do we enable children to be involved in the whole process, to experience the link between ideas and reality ?

Plans and diagrams for an outside area

The answer lies, I believe, in how you offer the vision and then support children through your planning to achieve their goals.

The use of outside areas and ways to create effective learning zones outside is detailed in the 'Potential of a Puddle' 2005, so this area of the book will look at ways in which we can help children see, use and plan in 2 and 3 dimensions. Children can use 2D - photographs, within a Talking Tub™ to look at landscape possibilities, smaller scale use of areas and resources.

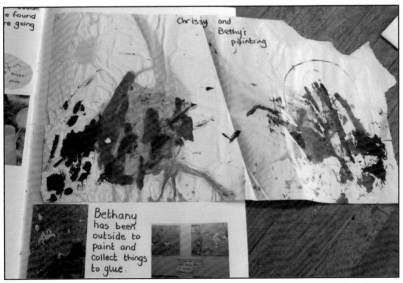

Children's thinking and experiences are integral to the book

Creating a vision of the possibilities

There is such a variety of styles of outside area that one blueprint will not adapt to them all. However if we focus on schemas such as enclosing and transporting, we can enable children to physically change any space with a few open-ended materials.

Enclosing space - enveloping themselves within dens and horizontal forms can be supported through the use of

Use bricks to enclose space, log slices can be used as a double path.

bricks, den building fabrics and be presented in a more permanent way through bushes in tubs, willow tunnels in window boxes and pods.

Log slices & rope are useful for lines and pathways

Transporting - the idea of travelling with and without objects can be supported through the use of log slices, paint markers, chalk, roll out paths, chains and rope to represent pathways and roads. Children will talk to you about where they want to go to and how they want to move.

An open area with core landscaping such as a small area of grass, mud, rock, a slope, hard-standing and higher vegetation gives a framework that children can change and adapt. Children can use wood shavings or mown grass to

create solid shapes that are often transformed into a type of directing.

Movable resources can be provided in response to children's interest, the method you use should reflect the methodology inside the centre. So, self help bags can contain small resources that children have suggested, such as 'ribbons for running', 'treasure to find' or 'rose petals for making perfume'. These ideas enter the planning sheet as a focus for adult interaction.

Wood shavings, sand and bark can be used to block in areas

- **Children can be active designers in early years centres.**
- **Adults should accept childrens work without changing it.**
- **Children have clear opinions about display.**

The Talking and Thinking Floorbooks™ can be used for all aspects of the curriculum, because of the nature of learning it will be holistic, with all areas of the curriculum weaving together throughout the book. In the example below from Morrison's Academy Nursery it was the creation of a new display that stimulated a talking and thinking experience that lead to some wonderful mathematical thinking.

A Crocodile Number Display

We asked the children what they would like to see on the display board. There were a lot of good ideas - one little boy felt very strongly that he wanted the board to have a crocodile with LOTS of teeth! This idea appealed to the majority of children and they became very enthusiastic about crocodiles and this led to a general discussion about the characteristics and habits of crocodiles and other reptiles. These ideas were recorded on paper and put into a Talking and Thinking Floorbook™.

The children were invited to help to plan the display. The adult structured the questions to keep the focus.

How long should the crocodile be?
Some stretched their arms as wide apart as they could, others suggested 50 metres, "69 metres", "5 metres", "as long as 5 children", "as big as a Daddy".

How many teeth should it have?
"542, "no 100", "2", "6", "lots", "millions", "no billions".

What colour should it be?
"Black", "green", "spotty", "camouflage …that is green and brown and blue so that it can hide near the water".

Sorting crocodile teeth

A large crocodile shape was created and the children worked out that they needed 6 people to help hold it! The children chose sponges to colour the body using green, black and brown colours. There was a discussion about how to mix colours, the size of the body, the length of the jaws, etc. All of the ideas were noted on a clipboard available in the area, so that we could transfer the information to our Talking and Thinking Book later in the session.

One child noted that the crocodile needed some teeth. The children drew the teeth onto thin card themselves and cut them out ……. big, small, crooked, sharp. A group of boys felt they needed to sort the teeth so arranged them on the table while talking about size and sharpness and comparing a dog's teeth to a lion's teeth. They stuck the teeth into the crocodile's jaws using their own sorting criteria, which resulted in a rather appealing crooked look !!

Their ideas and comments reflected their understanding of many mathematical concepts such as size, shape, number, tessellation,

"We need smaller teeth – right at the back"

"These are HUGE teeth"

"I got the hugest one"

"It's looking better – LOOK at all the teeth!"

"It's nearly full – room for a few – only 5 left"

" I think he has fifty hundred teeth"

"We need a tongue"

"Crocodiles don't have tongues"

" We could put a mouse in to get the bad tooth!"

Creating the crocodile

This little boy remembered a story about a mouse helping a crocodile by taking out a rotten tooth. He told the group about it and there was a discussion about being kind and helpful and sad and happy. He set off to go and draw the mouse to put into the crocodile's mouth.

One of the children brought along a reference book and pointed out that crocodiles have bumps on their backs. We decided that the bumps needed to be smaller on the thinner tail and bigger over the large stomach. Now these 'scales' needed sorting too, but the table was not long enough so the children pushed two tables together to make a very long table. Numbering the scales would be a good idea but the bigger numbers did not fit on the small scales. So make the little scales the smaller numbers and the bigger scales the larger numbers. We were able to number 21 scales ...a very BIG number!

How long is our crocodile? There were some wild guesses and we then discussed different ways of measuring it. Is he longer than a child? How many children would fit into the crocodile? For this we need to move the crocodile to the floor and then

Children meameasuring the crocodile

discovered we could fit 3 children into its length! One little boy felt we should use a tape measure and knew where to find one in the woodwork box. It was too short so we produced a second tape measure and they joined them up and read off lots of numbers.

Now the crocodile was finished and could be placed onto the display board. The children suggested and then helped to create grass, water and a sun for the board. We needed labels and again the children wrote out the words that interested them like crocodile, number, leg, sun, grass, water, jaw, mouse, and teeth. The connection to planning had to happen, since the children's plans were extensive and more engaging than the maths display we had in our minds.

By Nikki Buchan

• **Children are able to make decisions about some of the resources they wish to use.**
• **Open-ended resources enable children to be more creative and offer greater opportunities for planning to support learning.**

An Outdoor Den

In the nursery, each key group was encouraged to meet, talk and plan their ideas for the outdoor area. Each group took time to look at pictures of other areas, plants, colour charts, etc. so that they could have an informed discussion about what they wanted in their own outdoor area.

As is the practice with talking and thinking books, all the children's thinking was recorded through adult writing and this was supplemented with children's drawings/writing, photographs and pictures cut from magazines.

The types of features that children want often vary from those of adults. One group wanted to build a tongue coming out of the wall, to put the 'eating plants' in.
Another group wanted to hide squirrels, rabbits, moles and birds in the tree.
Another group wanted to be able to plant carrots, have a path that could move every day, have some sunshine, a flower – and a tree just for Morven.

Kildrum den

The most ambitious of the plans involved a den, which the group wanted to create. The key worker provided an old curtain and pegs and supported the group's wish to build a den around the tree. However, the curtain got wet and this stimulated discussion about more appropriate materials. The availability of a tarpaulin led the children to make a new roof. The den was used in that form for a week or so until an interest in Bob the Builder came through the talking and thinking books. Construction using hard materials was evident through the children's indoor play so the staff introduced large blocks, planks and tubing outdoors. It became evident from the children's play that they wanted to build a den that could 'stay up'.

The planning procedure started with rough sketches by individual children, to introduce the features that were important to them. The children wanted a chimney on the very top of the roof, a bird house at each side of the house, windows that they could open, a hole for a Christmas tree cable, seats, decoration and a carpet.

The wonderful aspect of this particular planning exercise is that the nursery had a link with a person who builds sheds and dens, so the children's ideas were able to become a reality. The wiggly circles and boxes that the children drew actually became the window shapes, and the chimney was built in exactly the place that the children wanted it. The children decorated logs slices with metallic

paint, and painted tiles to hang around inside the den. They helped to put carpet inside and created their own set of 'rules' for using the den:

Take your shoes off as soon as you come in so carpet doesn't get dirty
No hitting, no pushing, no kicking and punching
No silly words like bottom (!)
Be kind and listen

The children used the den for the two years that they were at nursery, each group developing and adding new details to it to make it their own. Unfortunately the tree in the outdoor area has had to be cut down because vandals used it to climb into the area,

and a small fire they lit burnt some of the den. The children, who live locally, see this type of behaviour regularly and adjusted their play to include the 'time the den got burnt', as part of their role-play. The staff responded by putting in a pretend fire extinguisher.

The next steps for development are to invest in waterproof dungarees to extend the protection that nursery coats already offer; staff use their new wellingtons on a regular basis. The centre is moving towards making outdoor learning a daily opportunity.

These are some of the comments that the children made.
The comments were taken from the talking and thinking book and used as the focus for the design.

'Jake wants the den to have a roof, a door and a chimney (a birdhouse).'
'Dillon wants decorations inside like Santa's house. He said "I want tiles to paint on and a light".'
'Elaine wants the den to have wood and a stamper for everyone who listens, and a pen.'
'Grant wants decorations – silver ones – and balloons.'
'Caitlynn and Dillon want to make a Santa sign so he stops and leaves presents for them.'
'We need a wibbly window to see out'

- **The underlying methodology of the Eco-Schools approach is consultation with the participants**
- **The Talking and Thinking Floorbooks™ support all aspects of the approach**

Eco-schools is a programme of environmental improvement that is designed for centres and groups working with children. Groups are encouraged to examine a variety of elements in their practice such as waste minimisation, outdoor spaces, healthy eating, transport use, or litter. One of the key elements of the approach is the integration of children's views and ideas. The methodology behind the eco-schools is based on consultation and the integration of all the people who are influenced by the environment in which they are living.

Children choosing an aspect they wish to explore

The eco-schools programme for older children use a variety of structured meetings with a council made up from parents, staff and children. The group is encouraged to consult as many people as possible to identify the area of the programme they wish to focus on. The use of Talking and Thinking Books™ allows people to share the process of consultation with a wider audience. When groups are working to gain recognition for their work it is important to share the process the centre has gone through to identify joint goals and targets. One of the challenges that nurseries face when they are trying to show a transient process such as play or the talk that comes from it is the awareness that young children have of the process. There is no clear evidence that would be appropriate to use with young children. The Talking and Thinking Floorbooks™ do exactly this.

The Eco-Nursery Floorbooks show;

- ❖ initial ideas and perceptions,
- ❖ voting systems,
- ❖ adult engagement and general awareness
- ❖ physical changes to the recycling area or outside zone,
- ❖ parent consultation
- ❖ evidence of general improvement
- ❖ action plans created by the adults and children.

The element that challenges most groups is how we can consult children and give them the chance to offer their ideas and make informed choices. The use of talking tubs, consultation boards and photographs with Possible Lines of Development.

A Talking Tub™ to encourage children to talk about litter and recycling would include A tin, a magnet, plastic ring strap for cans, a model of a hedgehog, an old sock, a newspaper, a bottle, a plastic milk container. The tub often reveals that children are aware of a great deal if their family is engaging in the programmes that are running across the country.

Children will say "animals get their heads trapped in the plastic"

"I go to the tip with my dad"

"I like the big lorry that comes and squashes all the rubbish"

"We have a box in the garage fro bottles and they smash when I put them in"

These statements are recorded on the talking bubbles and included in the book.

The consultation boards can enable children to gather information so that they make informed choices. The parents noticeboard should do the same. Some parents have a limited awareness of the easy steps we can take to reduce our environmental footprint. Through consulting and involving them in the process the awareness of eco- schools moves from being centre focussed to being part of the community and culture.

Photographs with P.L.O.D.s could include pictures of recycling centres, art made from recycled materials, the machinery used to process the materials, children engaged in activities such as sorting junk, preparing healthy snack, or clearing up outside. These photographs are spread over the Talkaround Mat™ and children look at them to find one that interests them. This becomes the focus of the next session so that the discussions are based on child interest or knowledge.

The whole process of exploration and discussion is recorded in the Talking and Thinking Book™. The book can then become an integral part of the ongoing Eco display. Key points of discussion can then be revisited or highlighted at any point.

Eco display

- **The approach is inspiring parents, practitioners and children to play together in a creative way.**
- **It is sustainable when it becomes embedded in daily practice.**
- **Consistency across the team supports long term sustainability.**

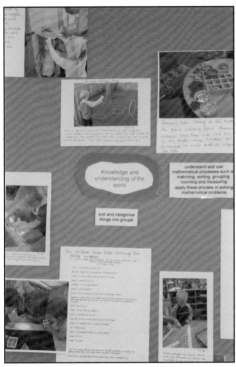

Displays to share thinking

The approach of a centre that is looking to change its practice in a significant way must be to consider how sustainable the overall development is. A commitment from the nursery team creates the most effective change, consistency is important within this approach, so that children feel secure in understanding the ethos and all the expectations that it brings with it.

The consultation of children will sit very easily within many people's personal beliefs, but for others they will need evidence and support that through letting go of the control over planning contexts and activities we can energise both our own practice and more importantly the children in our centres.

Displays that show the process of consultation to a wider audience such as parents, carers and visitors demonstrates the democratic ethos of the centre, where all children and their carers are valued citizens of the group. Programmes such as Eco-schools have taken on board the Talking and Thinking Floorbooks™ as a consultative approach to the information gathered through the pupil council and parent workshops.

How does it link to planning?

One of the key aspects about early years now is the increased paper work that endeavours to demonstrate breadth and balance in the curricular opportunities that we offer to children. In the process of accountability some planning grids look fabulous but have missed the connection between what they are providing and children's needs and interests. The Talking and Thinking Floorbooks™ should create a close link between children and the environment they are in.

Contexts for learning

If we imagine planning through consultation to be along a giant continuum, we can place our practice anywhere from "I don't do it at all", to "I consult on everything". The following examples move from higher direction and structure to minimal direction and a responsive structure.

- ❖ Adults decide that they will choose the context and then ask what children know about it through the Talking and Thinking Floorbooks™. The adult then plans from this what she/he will provide over the next few weeks.
- ❖ Adults choose the context, consult children about what they know and then go on to ask what the children would like to find out or use in the centre.

- ❖ Adults listen to children first, collate observations, find common threads and then offer a Talking Tub™ about the subject observed e.g. Ears.
- ❖ Adults consult children through the Talking and Thinking Floorbooks™ in a general way and, although they support individual children's ideas, also have an 'on offer activity.' That has been set up to stimulate play.
- ❖ Adults consult children and support a huge range of interests all of which can be explored through an open-ended resource provision. Stimulation and challenge are achieved through adult interaction and not planned activities.

Curricular links

There are a number of ways that we can record the curricular aspects of the books. In Scotland we work within the 3-5 curriculum, it should take two years to deliver and is flexible enough that many experiences cover a number of aspects. The curriculum can be delivered through just about any context or in fact where there is none at all, so many centres focus on curricular documents to monitor breadth and balance, not key learning linked to a specific context.

The curricular accountability for the centre can be achieved through;
- ❖ Printing a copy of the aspects of the curriculum and highlighting aspects explored through the book. This is done retrospectively and then attached into the back of the book.
- ❖ At the end of a key investigation or exploration, noting how the ideas and suggestions were implemented into practice and what aspects the play covered. The close timing between action and recording makes this accurate and detailed.
- ❖ Talking to children about the bigger picture supports metacognition. Revisiting the play experiences and pulling out significant learning gives children specific feedback that enables them to progress and challenge their existing frameworks of understanding. I might well sit for a short time with a key aspect in front of me, and obviously, whilst rephrasing the words, go through some simpler concepts with children. E.g. Alan, Laura, Colin and Kaz were playing with the fabrics in the den area and were looking at all the different types there were. What did you find out about the blue sheet?
  (Adult highlights properties and features of materials on a sheet in the Floorbook or separate file cross-referencing to floorbook)

Through using these techniques the adults monitor the breadth and balance of the curriculum. If there are aspects consistently being omitted the adult steps in to create an adult initiated activity or context through the Talking Tub™. This may be done towards the end of the year or throughout so that there is a woven integration of adult and child initiated opportunities.

Individual achievement

In order to monitor individual achievement most regions in Scotland support formative assessment. The Talking and Thinking Floorbooks™ obviously link directly with this. They also provide a group and centre progression that individual profiles cannot. Some centres have subdivided the key aspects of the 3-5 curriculum to make the statements of attainment more detailed. Some key group workers are monitoring the experiences in the books through these charts. If the paper work becomes too onerous the approach will lose flexibility just as in some adult initiated planning.

> ? • **Change is challenging, but worthwhile for the more effective teaching and learning environment that it creates.**

Any new approach will offer a few challenges in terms of confidence and understanding from both staff and children. Here are some of the challenges I have been posed in my travels delivering training across the world.

How do you get all the staff on board?
There are several ways to affect change in any establishment. One possibility is to direct by instruction and the other to lead through example. I choose the latter. Watching someone work with a group of children over a period of time enables people to see the long term sustainability of any approach. Given that, there should be a consistency of approach between rooms and across age groups so that children have clear understanding of what is expected of them.

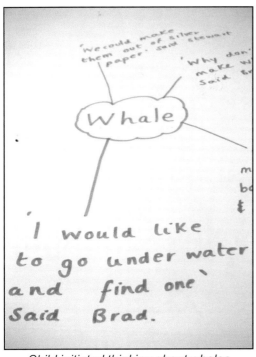

Child initiated thinking about whales

What do you do if they don't seem to know anything?
All children know something. The question is, is it what you want to hear? In order for this approach to work there has to be an acceptance of children's ideas and some of those ideas are phrased and formed very differently from an adult mind.
Consider the subject you are talking about, is it really relevant to them?

What subjects do they want to talk about?
The children we work with have only been on the planet for three years. In that time a year was semi-horizontal. So that leaves about 2 years for them to gather language, become mobile, to create a sense of emotional harmony and then start to understand the dynamics of a centre or perhaps just a new room. So consider what is close to them, about 75cm above the ground. A view that looks up to adults and anything taller than 75cm.!! They are close to the ground and that fascinates them, water, mud, grass all offer potential. Their size makes proportion slightly different, when they hold a snail, proportionally it is like you holding a snail that is 20cm long on your hand. No wonder they are fascinated. They may talk to you about things that they encounter outside the centre, television superheros like spider man can lead into wonderful discussions on how far he can swing, questions like " Does the rain hang on his web when it is left on the buildings?" "Do his arms hurt when he is hanging all day long?"

What do you do if the subject is always the same?
This approach is a partnership between a responsive adult and children. It does not mean that children do what they like all the time. As professionals we are there to monitor breadth and balance. Some of the Talking and Thinking Floorbooks are around

an adult initiation focus, others are from observation and discussion and therefore child focused. If at key points the adult feels that the group needs stimulation they set up a Talking Tub™ and then take up the ideas given by the children.

What do you do if a child won't speak?
Staff need to aware of the way that children communicate. In Scandinavian countries the staff are trained to read body language and non-verbal communication. It is something that we need to consider. Is the passive observer, or the elect mute learning very much? I would suggest that they are and that we need to find other ways for them to share their thinking. Some possibilities are photo boards to point to, smiley face stickers to show preference, or simple eye contact to acknowledge that they are with you.
It is possible that some children have met adults who de-valued what they were saying or gave it no status at all. In this instance we need to give positive feedback at every opportunity.

How do you have the time to write it all?
The books are created with the children rather than published after the event. Once children realise that we are slowing them down because they say so much and we cannot write fast enough, they seem to become more succinct in their answers. There needs to be a range of ways of collecting thoughts such as leaves on the Talking and Thinking tree, bubbles in the writing area, and the book itself in the book corner so the management of the situation is not pressured and uncomfortable. Not every syllable a child says is going to be recorded, interaction and activity are at the root of the approach. Record elements of talk that influence or adjust thinking.

What do you do with them all?
Children often revisit previous books to consider what other children have done in the same play environment. Since the photographs show a familiar environment and resources they are often immediately recognisable and allow children to make a more rapid connection from the book to activity. We do have a bank of books both for our reference but also for an increasing number of practitioners from centres wanting to take on board the approach to their planning.

The approach is dynamic and exciting, I really hope that you are inspired by what you have read. If you have any concerns or would like to talk over what you are doing, do contact me at the address detailed at the front of the book.